CAREERS FOR

COMPETITIVE SPIRITS

& Other Peak Performers

Careers for You Series

CAREERS FOR

COMPETITIVE SPIRITS

& Other Peak Performers

JAN GOLDBERG

SECOND EDITION

New York Chicago San Francisco Lisbon London Madrid Mexico City
Milan New Delhi San Juan Seoul Singapore Sydney Toronto

The *McGraw-Hill* Companies

Library of Congress Cataloging-in-Publication Data

Goldberg, Jan.
    Careers for competitive spirits & other peak performers / by Jan Goldberg.—
2nd ed.
            p.   cm. — (McGraw-Hill careers for you series)
        ISBN 0-07-146776-9 (alk. paper)
        1. Vocational guidance.   I. Title: Careers for competitive spirits and other
    peak performers.   II. Title.

    HF5382.G648 2007
    331.702—dc22   2006005825

1 2 3 4 5 6 7 8 9 0   DOC/DOC   0 9 8 7 6

ISBN-13: 978-0-07-146776-6
ISBN-10:   0-07-146776-9

McGraw-Hill books are available at special quantity discounts to use as premiums and
sales promotions, or for use in corporate training programs. For more information,
please write to the Director of Special Sales, Professional Publishing, McGraw-Hill,
Two Penn Plaza, New York, NY 10121-2298. Or contact your local bookstore.

This book is printed on acid-free paper.

This book is dedicated to my incredible husband, Larry, and my precious daughters, Sherri and Debbie. Thank you for bringing so much joy into my life.

Contents

Acknowledgments

The author gratefully acknowledges the following individuals for their contributions to this project:

- The numerous professionals who graciously agreed to be profiled in this book
- My dear husband, Larry, for his inspiration and vision
- My children, Deborah, Bruce, and Sherri, for their encouragement and love
- Family and close friends—Adrienne, Marty, Mindi, Cary, Michele, Paul, Michele, Alison, Steve, Marci, Steve, Brian, Steven, Jesse, Bertha, Uncle Bernard, and Aunt Helen—for their faith and support
- Diana Catlin for her insights and input

The editors would like to thank Josephine Scanlon, a freelance writer specializing in career topics, for preparing this revised edition.

Attention: Competitive Spirits

*A horse never runs so fast as when he has
other horses to catch up and outpace.*

—Ovid

Competitive spirits love a challenge. They perform at their best when they have deadlines to meet, quotas to break, competitors to beat. Obstacles are puzzles to be solved, problems to be overcome—not barriers blocking the way. No opposition is too large to tackle. In fact, the higher the stakes and the more difficult the rules, the greater the satisfaction for competitive types.

Most competitive spirits follow this credo in every facet of their lives—whether it's in the sports arena, vying for points; in educational institutions, competing for the highest grades; or on the job, striving for the best performance. When it comes to planning a professional career, competitive spirits know there is no greater thrill than putting their talents to the test and earning a living at the same time.

Competitive spirits approach a career choice with as much enthusiasm and forethought as they would any life challenge. True competitors plan ahead and make sure they know all their options. They study the rules and requirements of the game, become familiar with the playing field, and research the competition they'll face.

1

In the pages ahead you'll learn about a number of careers that might match your desire for a competitive atmosphere. Breaking in and rising to the top won't be a piece of cake for most of these careers, but that's the way competitive spirits like it. They don't want anything handed to them easily; they want to prove themselves and earn their successes every step of the way.

Do You Have What It Takes?

Before we examine the many options open to you, let's make sure you're a genuine peak performer who will thrive in a competitive atmosphere. Determine whether each of these statements is true or false in describing you:

1. The closer the deadline, the higher your energy level—and your productivity.
2. "Winner takes all" is your motto. No playing it safe and hedging your bets.
3. You want your paycheck to reflect your actual work output, to increase—or decrease—as a direct result of your efforts.
4. You think quickly on your feet.
5. You firmly believe that those who hesitate come in dead last.
6. You're always the first to know.
7. The words *I can't* are not in your vocabulary.
8. You thrive on pressure.
9. You work hard and play hard. Couch potatoes are the other guys.
10. You believe that no problem is insurmountable and that quitting is not an option.

Being the quick thinker that you are, you know that if each statement is true for you, it means you possess the personality, makeup, and qualities needed to do well in a competitive atmosphere. You've chosen this book because it's the right one for you.

You're on the right track, a winning track. Read on to learn more about a variety of career options.

....

Competitive Careers

Competitive spirits do well in any number of careers, but the ability to perform at a peak level isn't the only factor to consider. We all have our own special interests and areas where we excel. What follows is an overview of different careers where your ability to compete will be highly valued. Also included are possible settings in which you might find employment. But each position has its own requirements, working conditions, benefits, and downsides, and those will be discussed in detail in the chapters ahead.

Sales

No matter what they are selling—whether it is insurance, real estate, antiques, or exotic cars—sales professionals (in addition to being knowledgeable about their products) know how to interest customers in their merchandise. They have excellent verbal and written skills and are good at public speaking and giving convincing demonstrations. They also shine at social interaction, networking, and making contacts.

The income of many salespeople depends on the amount of business they bring in. Some are paid solely on a commission basis, earning a percentage for each product or service they sell. Other situations offer a salary plus commission. Often salespeople are rewarded with bonuses and extra perks, such as the use of a car and cell phone, for meeting and surpassing the quotas their employers set.

Possible Job Settings. Sales professionals work for many types of concerns and handle a variety of products and services. Retail sales run the gamut from department stores to specialty shops. You could sell automobiles or airplanes, washing machines or tractor trailers. Salespeople work in real estate, insurance, and the travel industry. Some sales teams work for manufacturers, wholesalers, and distributors, selling food to supermarkets and restaurants or expensive x-ray equipment to hospitals and doctors' offices.

Marketing

Marketing specialists are true strategists. As top executives or as team members, marketers determine the need and demand for products or services, identify potential customers, set appropriate prices to ensure a profit, and work on getting the word out to publicize their offerings. They work with other related professionals, including sales staff, product developers, public relations experts, advertisers, and promoters.

While developing a new product and watching it succeed can be very thrilling and rewarding, marketers can also risk losing their jobs if a product doesn't perform as predicted.

Possible Job Settings. Marketing professionals work within departments of large corporations or for small firms. They find their niche in advertising agencies or public relations firms. Employers can be anyone with a product, idea, or service to sell, and they range from educational institutions to the military.

Advertising

Advertising departments in large corporations or separate advertising firms usually focus on three main activities: account services, creative services, and media services.

The account services department assesses the need for advertising and maintains the accounts of clients. The creative services department develops the subject matter and the way the advertising is presented. This department is supervised by a creative director, who oversees the copy chief and art director and their staffs.

The media services department is supervised by the media director, who oversees planning groups that select the particular media in which the advertising will appear—for example, radio, television, newspapers, magazines, or outdoor signs.

All positions in advertising are fast paced, pressured, and extremely competitive. The bottom line is consumer dollars. Advertisers, along with a team of marketers, publicists, and sales staff, must vie with their competitors for every one of those dollars.

Possible Job Settings. Advertising specialists find work in many of the same settings as their marketing colleagues. Nonprofit associations, utility companies, government organizations, consulting firms, and educational facilities are just a few of the many possibilities in addition to the corporate world.

Public Relations

The public relations expert faces challenges every day, dealing mainly with the employer's image and the public's perception of it. Public relations professionals also help shape companies and the way they perform. By means of research and evaluation, PR practitioners find out the expectations and concerns of the public and report on their findings.

Public relations is a relatively young field, founded less than a hundred years ago. In the beginning, PR workers functioned more as press agents and publicists. As the profession grew and changed, those aspects became less the work of the PR professional and fell more into the realm of publicists and advertising and marketing professionals.

Today, the field of public relations encompasses a variety of job titles and professional responsibilities, including the consultant, the corporate communicator, the investor relations specialist, the public information officer, the community liaison, the government mediator, the troubleshooter, the spokesperson, and the media coordinator.

Possible Job Settings. PR professionals work in every sector, from the corporate world to the sporting world, from government departments to health and medical facilities. You'll find public relations specialists wherever there's an image to convey—or correct. Options include virtually every industry, from entertainment to travel, from food to health care. Labor unions, universities, state-owned corporations, publishing houses, and broadcasting companies all utilize the services of PR staff. And though the settings may vary, the backbone of every PR professional's job description is his or her role as communicator.

Law

Not every lawyer makes headline news, sets precedents for new laws, or gets to handle landmark cases. But even those working quietly, away from media attention, still feel the excitement of the game, the thrill of the chase, the satisfaction of a successful deal closing or the right verdict coming in.

And although not every law specialty provides the challenges that competitive spirits need, several do. This particularly includes criminal and trial law, both of which are worth considering as possible career choices.

Getting into law school is also a competitive process. Only those with the best grade point averages and LSAT (Law School Admission Test) scores make it. Once in, the workload for students can be overwhelming. Then there's the bar exam to pass and just the right law firm to land a job with.

On the job, challenges can arise every day, with briefs to research and write, arguments to put forward, battles to win or lose. Practicing law can be the perfect career choice for many peak performers.

Possible Job Settings. Lawyers can work for large or small private law firms or as in-house counsel for concerns such as banks, publishing companies, or a myriad of other corporations. Many legal experts work for the government as public defenders or prosecutors. However, the majority of lawyers work on their own in private practice.

Research

Just as reporters strive to get to the story first and land the big scoops, so do research scientists hope to be the first to discover medical cures or breakthrough technology. Funding is often limited and the pressure is high to produce results.

While images of the serious scientist working alone in a lab at a leisurely pace are often depicted in film and television, the reality is quite different. When funding dries up, sponsorship is withdrawn and jobs are lost if the research doesn't bear fruit.

In addition to possessing a competitive spirit, research scientists must have extensive training and in-depth knowledge of their field. They often spend years studying, earning master's and doctoral degrees, before landing full-time jobs. Income can be sporadic, based upon grants won and lost.

Possible Job Settings. Research scientists may find work in private or government-funded research labs, in medical schools and other university departments, in hospitals, and for pharmaceutical companies.

Entertainment

The entertainment world is a tough industry—there are plenty of talented people out there, and the competition for performance opportunities is stiff. Although *overnight success* is a catch phrase often tossed around, the truth is that most actors and musicians struggle for many years before even getting a role or having a song released, never mind a starring role or platinum album. Competitive spirits seeking a career in entertainment have to be thick-skinned as well as talented. Rejection is the name of the game.

Possible Job Settings. In addition to the three most obvious settings—the big screen, television, and stage—entertainers work in a variety of other environments, such as nightclubs or comedy clubs and private affairs such as weddings and bar mitzvahs. They may deliver singing telegrams, work as clowns or magicians at children's birthday parties, or train those who want to find a place in the entertainment industry.

Other Competitive Careers

There are a host of other competitive careers including (but not limited to) writing, reporting, professional sports, and politics. Sharpen your competitive edge by conducting an Internet search to find resources that provide information about some of these alternative careers.

Getting the Inside Scoop

What better way to learn about a profession than by talking to people who have worked in the field? A few phone calls to the right human resources department or the alumni office of your school can connect you with someone whose brain you can pick. Or you might arrange to follow someone around on the job for a day or two.

To better help you make an informed choice, several professionals have been interviewed within these pages. Their firsthand accounts tell you what their work involves, how they got started, and how you can enter the profession.

In addition, at the end of each chapter you will find the names and contact information of professional associations for many of the positions discussed in this book. Many list job openings within the field. Visit the websites to learn more about what each organization offers.

CHAPTER TWO

Careers in Sales

Everyone lives by selling something.
—Robert Louis Stevenson

For the competitive spirit, sales is often a natural career choice. In some areas of sales, your paycheck can directly reflect your effort. The harder you work and the more successful you are, the greater the financial reward. Sales professionals can compete with themselves and watch their checks increase from month to month. They can also compete with colleagues and win bonuses for having the highest sales in a given period.

In addition, the playing field spreads to competitors in similar businesses. Not only do sales professionals have to outdo themselves and other employees, they have to make sure their companies' products or services win out over the competition. Avis Car Rental's famous slogan, "We're #2. We try harder," is a great illustration of that point.

Areas of Specialty

The field of sales encompasses a wide range of job settings, products, and services, as well as methods of selling. Sales can be broken into the following three main categories:

- Retail
- Services
- Manufacturing and wholesale

There are also several sales categories that do not fit snugly into those three and have carved their own niches:

- Insurance sales
- Real estate sales
- Travel

Let's examine each of these competitive careers.

Retail Sales

Millions of dollars are spent each day on all types of merchandise—everything from sweaters and books to food and furniture. Whether selling clothing, cosmetics, or automobiles, a sales worker's primary job is to interest customers in the merchandise. This may be done by describing the product's features, demonstrating its use, showing various models and colors, and pointing out why products will benefit the customer or client.

Special knowledge and skills are needed for some jobs, particularly those that involve selling expensive and complex items. For example, workers who sell personal computers must be able to explain the features of various brands and models, the meaning of manufacturers' specifications, and the types of software that are available. In jobs selling standardized articles such as food, hardware, linens, and housewares, sales workers may often do little more than take payments and bag purchases.

Some retail sales workers also receive cash, check, and charge payments; handle returns; and give change and receipts. Depending on the hours they work, they may have to open or close the cash register, which may include counting the money in the cash register; separating charge slips, coupons, and exchange vouchers; and making deposits at the cash office. Sales workers are often held responsible for the contents of their registers, and, in many organizations, repeated shortages are cause for dismissal.

Sales workers may help stock shelves or racks, arrange for mailing or delivery of a purchase, mark price tags, take inventory, and prepare displays. Sales workers must be aware of the promotions their stores are sponsoring, as well as those that are being run by competitors. Also, they often must recognize possible security risks and know how to handle such situations.

Consumers often form their impressions of a store by its sales force. The retail industry is very competitive, and employers are increasingly stressing the importance of providing courteous and efficient service. For example, when a customer wants a product that is not available, the salesperson may place a special order or call another store to locate the item.

Job Settings

Sales workers are employed by many types of retailers to assist customers in the selection and purchase of merchandise. The largest employers of retail sales workers are department stores. Other types of employers include specialty shops, boutiques, independently owned stores, and large chain outlets, such as those selling hardware or office supplies. Catalog and online sales are two additional avenues for those interested in sales careers.

Training and Qualifications

Usually, there are no formal education requirements for this type of work. Employers look for candidates who enjoy working with people and have the tact and patience to deal with difficult customers. Among other desirable characteristics are an interest in sales, a neat appearance, and the ability to communicate clearly and effectively. Before hiring, some employers conduct background checks, especially for jobs involving high-priced items. Drug screening is also a common practice.

In most small stores, an experienced employee or the proprietor instructs newly hired sales personnel in making out sales checks and operating the cash register. In larger stores, training programs are more formal and usually are conducted over several days.

As salespeople gain experience and seniority, they usually move to positions of greater responsibility and are given their choice of departments, which can mean moving to areas with potentially higher earnings and commissions. The highest earning potential is usually found selling big-ticket items, work that often requires the most knowledge of the product and the greatest talent for persuasion.

In years past, capable sales workers without a college degree could advance to management positions, but today's large retail businesses generally prefer to hire college graduates as management trainees, making a college education increasingly important. Despite this trend, capable employees without a degree should still be able to advance to administrative or supervisory work in large stores.

Opportunities for advancement vary in small stores. In some establishments, advancement is limited because one person, often the owner, does most of the managerial work. In others, however, some sales workers are promoted to assistant managers.

Retail selling experience may be an asset when applying for sales positions with larger retailers or in other industries, such as financial services, wholesale trade, or manufacturing.

Earnings in Retail Sales

The starting salary for many part-time retail sales positions is the federal minimum wage. In some areas where employers have difficulty attracting and retaining workers, wages are much higher than the established minimum.

Compensation systems vary by type of establishment and merchandise sold. Some sales workers receive an hourly wage; others receive a commission or a combination of wages and commissions. Under a commission system, salespeople receive a percentage of the sales they make. These systems offer the opportunity to significantly increase earnings, but sales workers may find their earnings depend as much on the ups and downs in the economy as on their ability to sell their products.

Median hourly earnings of retail salespeople, including commissions, were $8.98 in 2004. The middle 50 percent earned between $7.46 and $12.22 an hour. The lowest 10 percent earned less than $6.38, and the highest 10 percent earned more than $17.85 an hour. Median hourly earnings in the industries employing the largest numbers of retail salespeople were as follows:

Automobile dealers	$18.61
Building material and supplies dealers	$10.85
Department stores	$8.47
Other general merchandise stores	$8.36
Clothing stores	$8.17

In addition, nearly all sales workers are able to buy store merchandise at a discount, often from 10 to 40 percent below regular prices. In some cases, this privilege is extended to the employees' families as well.

Services Sales

Services sales representatives sell a wide variety of services. For example, sales representatives for data processing services firms sell complex services such as inventory control, payroll processing, sales analysis, and financial reporting systems. Hotel sales representatives contact government, business, and social groups to solicit convention and conference business for the hotel.

Fund-raisers plan programs to raise money for charities or other nonprofit causes. Sales representatives for temporary help services firms locate and acquire clients to hire the firm's employees. Telephone services sales representatives visit commercial customers to review their telephone systems, analyze their communications needs, and recommend services, such as installation of additional equipment. Other representatives sell automotive leasing, public utility, burial, shipping, protective, and management consulting services.

Services sales representatives act as industry experts, consultants, and problem solvers when selling a firm's services. In some cases, the sales representative creates demand for the firm's services. A prospective client who is asked to consider buying a particular service may never have used, or even been aware of a need for, that service. For example, wholesalers persuaded to order a list of credit ratings to check their customers' credit prior to making sales might discover that the list could be used to solicit new business.

There are several different categories of services sales jobs:

- **Outside sales representatives** call on clients and prospects at their homes or offices. They may have an appointment, or they may make cold calls, which means arriving without an appointment.
- **Inside sales representatives** work on company premises, assisting individuals interested in the company's services.
- **Telemarketing sales representatives** sell exclusively over the telephone. They make large numbers of calls to prospects, attempting to sell company services themselves or to arrange appointments between the prospects and an outside sales representative. Some sales representatives deal exclusively with one, or a few, major clients.

Despite the diversity of services being sold, the jobs of all services sales representatives have much in common. All sales representatives must fully understand and be able to discuss the services their companies offer. Also, the procedures they follow are similar. Many sales representatives develop lists of prospective clients through telephone and business directories, ask business associates and customers for leads, and call on new businesses as they cover their assigned territories. Some services sales representatives acquire clients through customer inquiries.

Regardless of how they first meet the client, all services sales representatives must explain how the services being offered can meet client needs. This often involves demonstrations of company services. Sales representatives must answer questions about the nature and cost of the services and try to overcome objections in order to persuade potential customers to purchase the services. If they fail to make a sale on the first visit, they may follow up with additional visits, letters, or phone calls. After closing a sale, representatives generally follow up to see that the purchase meets the customer's needs and to determine whether additional services can be sold.

Because services sales representatives obtain many of their new accounts through referrals, success hinges on developing a satisfied clientele who will continue to use the services and will recommend them to other potential customers. Like other types of sales jobs, a services sales representative's reputation is crucial to his or her success.

Services sales work varies with the kind of service sold. Selling highly technical services, such as communications systems or computer consulting services, involves complex and lengthy sales negotiations. In addition, sales of such complex services may require extensive after-sale support. In these situations, sales representatives may operate as part of a team of sales representatives and experts from other departments who provide valuable technical assistance. For example, those who sell data processing services might work with a systems engineer or computer scientist, and those who sell telephone services might receive technical assistance from a communications consultant. Teams enhance customer service and build strong, long-term relationships with customers, resulting in increased sales.

Because of the length of time between the initial contact with a customer and the actual sale, representatives who sell complex technical services generally work with several customers simultaneously. For this reason, they must be well organized and efficient in scheduling their time. Selling less complex services, such as linen supply or exterminating services, generally involves simpler and shorter sales negotiations.

A sales representative's job may likewise vary with the size of the employer. Those working for large companies generally are more specialized and are assigned territorial boundaries, a specific line of services, and their own accounts. In smaller companies, sales representatives may have broader responsibilities: administrative, marketing, or public relations, for example, in addition to their sales duties.

Job Settings

Services sales representatives hold more than five hundred thousand jobs nationwide. More than half work for firms providing business services, including computer and data processing, advertising, personnel supply, equipment rental and leasing, mailing, reproduction, and stenographic services.

Other sales representatives work for firms that offer a wide range of services, such as business services (advertising, computer and data processing, personnel supply, mailing), engineering and management, personal, amusement and recreation, automotive repair, membership organizations, hotels, motion pictures, health, and education.

Training and Qualifications

Many employers require services sales representatives to have a college degree, but requirements may vary depending on the industry a particular company represents. Employers who market advertising services seek individuals with a bachelor's degree in advertising or marketing or a master's degree in business administration; companies that market educational services prefer individuals with an advanced degree in marketing or a related field.

Many hotels seek graduates from college hotel administration programs, and companies that sell computer services and telephone systems prefer sales representatives with a background in computer science or engineering. College courses in business, economics, communications, and marketing are helpful in obtaining other jobs as services sales representatives.

Employers may hire experienced, high-performing sales representatives who have only a high school diploma. This is particularly true for those who sell nontechnical services, such as exterminating, laundry, or funeral services.

Many firms conduct intensive training programs for their sales representatives. A sound training program covers the history of the business; origin, development, and uses of the service; effective prospecting methods; presenting the service; answering customer objections; creating customer demand; closing a sale; writing an order; understanding company policies; and using technical support personnel.

Sales representatives also may attend seminars on a wide range of subjects given by in-house or outside training institutions. These sessions acquaint employees with new services and products, help them maintain and update their sales techniques, and may include motivational or sensitivity training to make sales representatives more effective in dealing with people. Sales staffs generally receive training in the use of computers and communications technology in order to increase their productivity.

To be successful, sales representatives should have pleasant, outgoing personalities and good rapport with people. They must be highly motivated, well organized, and efficient. Good grooming and a neat appearance are essential, as are self-confidence, reliability, and the ability to communicate effectively. Sales representatives should be self-starters who can work under pressure to meet sales goals.

Sales representatives who have good sales records and leadership ability may advance to supervisory and managerial positions. Frequent contact with businesspeople in other firms provides sales workers with leads about job openings, enhancing advancement opportunities.

Earnings for Services Sales Representatives

The average yearly income for entry-level sales positions is about $36,000, ranging up to $63,000 for senior sales staff. Earnings of experienced sales representatives depend on performance. Successful sales representatives who establish a strong customer base can sometimes earn more than their managers. Some sales representatives earn well over $100,000 a year.

Sales representatives work on different types of compensation plans. Some receive a straight salary; others are paid solely on a commission basis—a percentage of the dollar value of their sales. Most firms use a combination of salary and commission.

Some services sales representatives receive a base salary plus incentive pay that adds 50 to 70 percent to the base salary, based on their performance. In addition to the same benefits package received by other employees of the firm, outside sales representatives have expense accounts to cover meals and travel, and some drive a company car. Many employers offer bonuses, including vacation time, trips, and prizes, for sales that exceed company quotas.

Earnings of representatives who sell technical services generally are higher than earnings of those who sell nontechnical services. In spite of all the perks, with fluctuating economic conditions and consumer and business expectations, earnings may vary widely from year to year.

Manufacturers' and Wholesale Sales

Articles of clothing, books, and computers are among the thousands of products bought and sold each day, and manufacturers' and wholesale sales representatives play an important role in this process. While retail sales workers sell products directly to customers, manufacturers' representatives market company products to other manufacturers, wholesale and retail establishments, government agencies, and institutions. Regardless of the kinds of products they sell, the primary duties of these sales representatives are to interest wholesale and retail buyers and purchasing agents in their merchandise and to ensure that any questions or concerns of current clients are addressed. Sales reps also provide advice to clients on how to increase their retail sales.

Job titles in this field differ depending on the employment setting. Those representing manufacturers are referred to as manufacturers' representatives, and those employed by wholesalers generally are called sales representatives. Representatives who sell technical products, for both manufacturers and wholesalers, are usually called industrial sales workers or sales engineers. Rather than working directly for a firm, some manufacturers' agents are self-employed sales workers who contract their services to all types of companies.

Manufacturers' and wholesale sales representatives spend much of their time traveling to and visiting with prospective buyers and current clients. During a sales call, they discuss the customers' needs and suggest how their products or services can meet those needs. They may show samples or catalogs that describe items their companies stock and inform customers about prices, availability, and how their products can save money and improve productivity. In addition, because of the vast number of manufacturers and wholesalers selling similar products, they try to beat competitors by emphasizing the unique qualities of the products and services offered by their companies. They also take orders and resolve any problems or complaints with the products and services.

These sales representatives have additional duties as well. For example, sales engineers, who are among the most highly trained sales workers, typically sell products that require technical expertise to install and use. Sales engineers may also need to familiarize their clients with support products for their purchases, such as material-handling equipment, numerical-control machinery, and computer systems.

In addition to providing information about the firms' products, these workers help prospective and current buyers with technical problems. For example, sales engineers might recommend improved materials and machinery for a firm's manufacturing process, draw up plans of proposed machinery layouts, estimate cost savings from the use of their equipment, and negotiate the sale—a process that may take several months.

Sales engineers must also provide follow-up services, keeping close contact with clients to ensure that they renew their contracts. Sales engineers may work with engineers in their own companies, adapting products to special customer needs.

Increasingly, sales representatives who lack technical expertise work as a team with a technical expert. For example, sales representatives make the preliminary contacts with customers, introduce their products, and close the sales. Technical representatives attend the sales presentations to explain the products and answer technical questions and concerns. In this way, the sales representative is able to spend more time maintaining and soliciting accounts and less time acquiring and conveying technical knowledge.

Obtaining new accounts is an important part of the job. Sales representatives follow leads from other clients, from advertisements in trade journals, and from participation in trade shows and conferences. At times, they make unannounced visits to potential clients. In addition, they may spend a lot of time meeting with and entertaining prospective clients during evenings and weekends.

Sales representatives also analyze sales statistics, prepare reports, and handle administrative duties, such as filing their expense account reports, scheduling appointments, and making travel plans. They study literature about new and existing products and monitor the products, prices, and sales of their competitors. Supervisors track the daily activities of sales reps—where they have been, whom they have seen, and what they have sold.

Some manufacturers' and wholesale sales representatives have large territories and do considerable traveling. Because a sales region may cover several states, they may be away from home for several days or weeks at a time. Others work near their home bases and do most of their traveling by automobile. Because of the nature of the work and the amount of travel, sales representatives typically work more than forty hours per week.

Sales Managers

Sales managers direct their firms' sales programs. They assign sales territories and goals and establish training programs for their sales representatives. Managers advise their sales representatives on ways to improve their sales performance. In large, multiproduct firms, they oversee regional and local sales managers and their staffs. Sales managers maintain contact with dealers and distributors. They analyze sales statistics gathered by their staffs to determine sales potential and inventory requirements and monitor the preferences of customers, information that is vital to developing products and maximizing profits.

To operate as efficiently as possible, sales managers go out in the field to see their sales representatives, rather than having the reps take time away from clients by coming to the office. They also make sure the reps are using the right techniques in order to maximize sales.

Training and Qualifications

The background needed for sales jobs varies by product line and market. As the number of college graduates has increased and the job requirements have become more technical and analytical, most firms have placed a greater emphasis on a strong educational background. Nevertheless, many employers still hire individuals with previous sales experience who do not have college degrees. In fact, for some consumer products, sales ability, personality, and familiarity with brands are more important than a degree.

On the other hand, firms selling industrial products often require degrees in science or engineering in addition to some sales experience. In general, companies are looking for the best and brightest individuals who have the personal characteristics and desire necessary to sell.

Many companies provide formal training programs for beginning sales representatives that last up to two years. However, most businesses are accelerating these programs to reduce costs and to expedite the return on the investment in training. In some programs, trainees rotate among jobs in plants and offices to learn all phases of production, installation, and distribution of the products. In others, trainees may take formal classroom instruction at the plant, followed by on-the-job training under the supervision of a field sales manager.

In some firms, new workers are trained by accompanying more experienced workers on their sales calls. As these workers gain familiarity with the firm's products and clients, they are given increasing responsibility until they are eventually assigned their own territories. As businesses experience greater competition, increased pressure is placed upon sales representatives to be more productive. They also must stay abreast of new merchandise and the changing needs of their customers.

Sales representatives should enjoy traveling because much of their time is spent visiting current and prospective clients. They may attend trade shows where new products are displayed or conferences and conventions where they meet with other sales representatives and clients to discuss new product developments. In addition, many companies sponsor meetings for the entire sales force to discuss sales performance, product development, and profitability.

Earnings for Manufacturers' and Wholesale Sales Representatives

Compensation methods vary significantly by the type of firm and the products sold. However, most employers use a combination of salary and commission or salary plus bonus. Commissions are usually based on the total amount of sales, whereas bonuses may depend on individual performance, on the performance of all sales workers in the group or district, or on the company's performance.

Median annual earnings for full-time manufacturers' and wholesale sales representatives average between $45,000 and $58,000, although some might start as low as $24,000 and others earn well over $100,000. Earnings vary by experience and geographic region.

Manufacturers' and wholesale sales representatives are generally split into two categories—those who sell technical and scientific products and those who sell nontechnical and nonscientific products. The industries that employ the largest numbers of sales representatives of technical and scientific products are computer systems design and related services, wholesale electronic markets and agents and brokers, drugs and druggists' sundries merchant wholesalers, professional and commercial equipment and supplies merchant wholesalers, and electrical and electronic goods merchant wholesalers.

The industries employing the largest numbers of workers selling nontechnical and nonscientific products are wholesale electronic markets and agents and brokers; machinery, equipment, and supplies merchant wholesalers; professional and commercial equipment and supplies merchant wholesalers; grocery and related product wholesalers; and miscellaneous nondurable goods merchant wholesalers.

In addition to their earnings, sales representatives are usually reimbursed for expenses, including transportation costs, meals, hotels, and entertaining customers. They often receive benefits, such as health and life insurance, a pension plan, vacation and sick leave, personal use of a company car, and frequent-flyer mileage. Some companies offer additional incentives, such as free vacation trips or gifts for outstanding sales.

Unlike sales reps working directly for a manufacturer or wholesaler, manufacturers' agents work strictly on commission. Depending on the types of products they sell, their levels of experience in the field, and the number of clients they have, their earnings can vary significantly. In addition, because manufacturers' agents are self-employed, they must pay their own travel and entertainment expenses as well as provide for their own benefits, which can be expensive. Frequently, promotion takes the form of an assignment to a larger account or territory where commissions are likely to be greater.

Experienced sales representatives may move into jobs training new employees on selling techniques and company policies and procedures. Those who have good sales records and leadership abilities may advance to sales supervisor or district manager. Others find opportunities in buying, purchasing, advertising, or marketing research. For many sales reps, the end goal is to climb the ladder in sales and transfer into marketing.

Insurance Sales

Most people have their first contact with an insurance company through an insurance sales agent. These workers help individuals, families, and businesses select insurance policies that provide the best protection for their lives, health, and property. Agents prepare reports, maintain records, seek out new clients, and, in the event of a loss, help policyholders settle their insurance claims. Increasingly, some are also offering their clients financial analysis or advice on ways the clients can minimize risk.

Insurance sales agents sell one or more types of insurance, such as property and casualty, life, health, disability, and long-term care. Property and casualty insurance agents sell policies that protect individuals and businesses from financial loss resulting from automobile accidents, fire, theft, storms, and other events that can damage property. For businesses, property and casualty insurance can also cover injured workers' compensation, product liability claims, or medical malpractice claims. Life insurance agents specialize in selling policies that pay beneficiaries when a policyholder dies, as well as annuities that promise a retirement income. Health insurance agents sell policies that cover the costs of medical care and loss of income due to illness or injury. They also may sell dental insurance and short- and long-term disability insurance policies.

An increasing number of insurance sales agents offer comprehensive financial planning services to their clients, such as retirement planning, estate planning, or assistance in setting up pension plans for businesses. As a result, many insurance agents are involved in "cross-selling" or "total account development." Besides offering insurance, these agents may become licensed to sell mutual funds, variable annuities, and other securities. This practice is most common with life insurance agents who already sell annuities; however, property and casualty agents also sell financial products.

Technology has greatly affected the insurance agency, making it much more efficient and giving agents the ability to take on more clients. Agents' computers are now linked directly to insurance carriers via the Internet, making the tasks of obtaining price quotes and processing applications and service requests faster and easier. Computers also allow agents to be better informed about new products that the insurance carriers may be offering.

Because insurance sales agents also obtain many new accounts through referrals, it is important that they maintain regular contact with their clients to ensure that the clients' financial needs are being met. Developing a satisfied clientele that will recommend an agent's services to other potential customers is a key to success in this field.

Training and Qualifications
For insurance sales agent jobs, most companies and independent agencies prefer to hire college graduates, especially those who have majored in business or economics. High school graduates are occasionally hired if they have proven sales ability or have been successful in other types of work. In fact, many entrants to insurance sales jobs transfer from other occupations. In selling commercial insurance, technical experience in a particular field can

help sell policies to those in the same profession. As a result, new agents tend to be older than entrants in many other occupations.

College training may help agents grasp the technical aspects of insurance policies and the fundamentals and procedures of selling insurance. Many colleges and universities offer courses in insurance, and a few schools offer a bachelor's degree in the field. College courses in finance, mathematics, accounting, economics, business law, marketing, and business administration help insurance sales agents understand how social and economic conditions relate to the insurance industry. Courses in psychology, sociology, and public speaking can prove useful in improving sales techniques. Familiarity with computers and popular software packages has become very important because computers provide instantaneous information on a wide variety of financial products.

Insurance sales agents must be licensed by the state where they plan to work. Separate licenses are required for agents to sell life and health insurance and property and casualty insurance. In most states, licenses are issued only to applicants who complete specified prelicensing courses and who pass state examinations covering insurance fundamentals and state insurance laws. The insurance industry is increasingly moving toward uniform state licensing standards and reciprocal licensing, allowing agents who earn a license in one state to become licensed in other states upon passing the appropriate courses and examination.

A number of organizations offer professional designation programs that certify one's expertise in specialties such as life, health, and property and casualty insurance, as well as financial consulting. For example, the National Alliance for Education and Research offers a wide variety of courses in health, life, and property and casualty insurance for independent insurance agents. Although voluntary, such programs assure clients and employers that an agent has a thorough understanding of the relevant specialty. Agents are usually required to complete a specified number of hours of continuing education to retain the designations.

Given the diversity of financial products sold by insurance agents today, employers are also placing greater emphasis on continuing professional education. It is important for insurance agents to keep current on issues concerning their clients. Changes in tax laws, government benefits programs, and other state and federal regulations can affect the insurance needs of clients and the way agents conduct business. Agents can enhance their selling skills and broaden their knowledge of insurance and other financial services by attending institutes, conferences, and seminars sponsored by insurance organizations. Most state licensing authorities also have mandatory continuing education requirements focusing on insurance laws, consumer protection, and the technical details of various insurance policies.

Insurance sales agents should be flexible, enthusiastic, confident, disciplined, hard working, and willing to solve problems. They should communicate effectively and inspire customer confidence. Because they usually work without supervision, sales agents must be able to plan their time well and have the initiative to locate new clients.

An insurance sales agent who shows ability and leadership may become a sales manager in a local office. A few advance to agency superintendent or executive positions. However, many who have built up a good clientele prefer to remain in sales work. Some agents, particularly in the property and casualty field, establish their own independent agencies or brokerage firms.

Training for Insurance Agents in Canada

Entry into insurance sales usually requires at least secondary school graduation and completion of provincial licensing requirements. Graduation from a program in business administration or financial management or a bachelor's degree in an area of arts or science is often an asset.

On-the-job training and insurance industry courses and training programs are standard requirements. In addition, licensing by the insurance governing body in the province or territory of employment is required.

Earnings for Insurance Salespeople

Many independent agents are paid by commission only, whereas sales workers who are employees of an agency or an insurance carrier may be paid in one of three ways—salary only, salary plus commission, or salary plus bonus. In general, commissions are the most common form of compensation, especially for experienced agents. The amount of the commission depends on the type and amount of insurance sold and on whether the transaction is a new policy or a renewal.

Bonuses usually are awarded when agents meet their sales goals or when an agency meets its profit goals. Some agents involved with financial planning receive a fee for their services, rather than a commission.

The median annual earnings of insurance sales agents were $41,720 in 2004. The middle 50 percent earned between $29,980 and $66,160. The lowest 10 percent had earnings of $23,170 or less, while the highest 10 percent earned more than $108,800. Median annual earnings in the two industries employing the largest number of insurance sales agents were $42,010 for insurance carriers and $41,840 for agencies, brokerages, and other insurance-related activities.

Company-paid benefits to insurance sales agents usually include continuing education, training to qualify for licensing, group insurance plans, office space, and clerical support services. Some companies also may pay for automobile and transportation expenses, attendance at conventions and meetings, promotion and marketing expenses, and retirement plans. Independent agents working for insurance agencies receive fewer benefits, but their commissions may be higher to help them pay for marketing and other expenses.

Real Estate Sales

Buying or selling a home or an investment property is not only one of the most important financial events in peoples' lives, but one of the most complex transactions as well. As a result, people generally seek the help of real estate agents or brokers to complete these transactions.

Real estate agents and brokers need to have a thorough knowledge of the housing market in their communities. They must know which neighborhoods will best fit their clients' needs and budgets. They have to be familiar with local zoning and tax laws and know where to obtain financing. Agents and brokers also negotiate price between buyers and sellers.

Career Opportunities

Brokers. Brokers are independent businesspeople who sell real estate owned by others; they also may rent or manage properties for a fee. When selling real estate, brokers arrange for title searches and for meetings between buyers and sellers during which the details of the transactions are agreed upon and the new owners take possession of the property. A broker may help the prospective buyer to arrange favorable financing from a lender; often, this makes the difference between success and failure in closing a sale.

In some cases, brokers and agents assume primary responsibility for closing sales; in others, lawyers or lenders do. Brokers supervise agents who may have many of the same job duties. Brokers also supervise their own offices, advertise properties, and handle other business matters.

Agents. Real estate agents usually are independent sales workers who provide their services to a licensed broker on a contract basis. In return, the broker pays the agent a portion of the commission earned from the agent's sale of the property.

Responsibilities of Real Estate Professionals

When working with customers in real estate, the most important thing an agent does is to listen to their needs. It is not uncommon for clients to describe a dream home that is actually more expensive than they can afford. The agent's job begins with helping the clients to determine their priorities. Do they really need four bedrooms, for example, or will three do? Do they want one story or two? Do they need a room to serve as an office?

At this point, the agent or broker consults a mortgage broker to determine the clients' financial situation. This prequalification phase is very important, since it tells both the agent and the clients how much the clients can afford to pay for a property.

Next the agent searches databases to find properties in the clients' price range. It is important for the agent to be well aware of the customers' needs and desires so that time is not wasted in showing properties that the clients are not interested in.

Then, the house hunting begins. Agents spend a lot of time showing homes to prospective buyers. Once a home has been found and the contract has been signed by both parties, the real estate broker or agent must ensure that all special terms of the contract are met before the closing date. For example, if the seller has agreed to a home inspection or termite and radon inspections, the agent must make sure that they are done. Sometimes these inspections reveal needed repairs; if the seller has agreed to make repairs, the broker or agent must see to it that they are completed satisfactorily before the sale can close.

Increasingly, brokers and agents must handle environmental problems or make sure the properties they are selling meet environmental regulations. For example, they may be responsible for dealing with problems such as lead paint on the walls. While many other details are handled by loan officers, attorneys, or other people, the agent must check to make sure that they are completed.

Because brokers and agents must have properties to sell, they spend a significant amount of time obtaining listings (owner agreements to place properties for sale with the firm). They spend much time on the telephone exploring leads gathered from various sources, including personal contacts. When listing properties for sale, agents and brokers make comparisons with similar properties that have been sold recently to determine fair market value.

Most real estate agents and brokers sell residential property. A few, usually those from large firms or specialized small firms, sell commercial, industrial, agricultural, or other types of real estate. Each specialty requires knowledge of that particular kind of property and clientele.

Although real estate agents and brokers generally work in offices, much of their time is spent showing properties to customers, analyzing properties for sale, meeting with prospective clients, researching the state of the market, inspecting properties for appraisal, and performing a wide range of other duties. Brokers provide office space, but agents generally furnish their own automobiles.

Training and Qualifications

Real estate agents and brokers must be licensed in every state and the District of Columbia. Prospective agents must be high school graduates, at least eighteen years old, and must pass a written test. The examination includes questions on basic real estate transactions and laws affecting the sale of property. The exam for brokers is more comprehensive than that for agents. Most states require candidates for the general sales license to complete between thirty and ninety hours of classroom instruction. Candidates for a broker's license need between sixty and ninety hours of formal training and a specific amount of experience selling real estate, usually one to three years. Some states waive the experience requirements for the broker's license for applicants who have a bachelor's degree in real estate.

State licenses typically must be renewed every one or two years; usually, no examination needs to be taken. However, many states require continuing education for license renewals. Exact licensing requirements are available from the real estate licensing commission of each state.

As real estate transactions have become more legally complex, many firms have turned to college graduates to fill positions. College courses in real estate, finance, business administration, statistics, economics, law, and English are helpful. For those who intend to start their own companies, business courses such as marketing and accounting are as significant as courses in real estate or finance.

In this highly interactive field, personality traits can be as important as academic background. Brokers look for agents who possess a pleasant personality, are honest, and present a neat appearance. Maturity, good judgment, trustworthiness, and enthusiasm for the job are required in order to encourage prospective customers in this highly competitive field. Agents should be well organized, be detail oriented, and have a good memory for names, faces, and business particulars.

Many firms offer formal training programs for both beginners and experienced agents. Larger firms usually offer more extensive programs than smaller firms. More than a thousand universities, colleges, and junior colleges offer courses in real estate. At some, a student can earn an associate's or bachelor's degree with a major in real estate; several offer advanced degrees. Many local real estate associations that are members of the National Association of Realtors sponsor courses covering the fundamentals and legal aspects of the field. Advanced courses in mortgage financing, property development and management, and other subjects also are available.

Advancement opportunities for agents may take the form of higher rates of commission. As agents gain knowledge and expertise, they become more efficient in closing a greater number of transactions and thereby increase their earnings. In many large firms, experienced agents can advance to sales manager or general manager. Those who have received a broker's license may open their own offices. Others with experience and training in estimating property value may become real estate appraisers, and people familiar with operating and maintaining rental properties may become property managers. Experienced agents and brokers with a thorough knowledge of business conditions and property values in their localities may enter mortgage financing or real estate investment counseling.

Training for Real Estate Agents in Canada

According to the Canadian Real Estate Association, education and licensing requirements for jobs in the real estate industry are established by the individual provinces. Aspiring agents and brokers should check the requirements of the province in which they intend to sell real estate.

In most provinces, educational requirements must be met before one can enter the field. A period of supervised practical training, sometimes called articling, may also be required before a worker can be registered as a real estate professional.

Colleges and universities offer a variety of real estate or related courses. At many of these colleges, students can specialize in a program that leads to a bachelor's degree in real estate. Some universities offer graduate-level courses. Continuing education is also required in many provinces so that real estate professionals can stay current on the issues that affect the industry.

Provincial licensing is required throughout the country. Although licensing requirements vary, all provinces and territories require prospective salespeople and brokers to pass a written exam.

Earnings for Real Estate Agents and Brokers

Commissions on sales are the main source of earnings of real estate agents and brokers. The rate of commission varies according to what the agent and broker agree on, the type of property, and its value. The percentage paid on the sale of farm and commercial properties or unimproved land is typically higher than the percentage paid for selling a home.

Commissions may be divided among several agents and brokers. When a property is sold, the broker or agent who obtained the listing usually shares the commission with the broker or agent who made the sale and with the firm that employs each of them. Although an agent's share varies greatly from one firm to another, often it is about half of the total amount received by the firm. Agents who both list and sell a property therefore maximize their commissions.

The median annual earnings of salaried real estate sales agents, including commissions, were $35,670 in 2004. The middle 50 percent earned between $23,500 and $58,110 a year. The lowest 10 percent earned less than $17,600, and the highest 10 percent earned more than $92,770. The industries that employed the highest numbers of real estate agents were residential building construction, offices of real estate agents and brokers, activities related to real estate, and companies that lease real estate.

Median annual earnings of salaried real estate brokers, including commission, were $58,720 in 2004. The middle 50 percent earned between $33,480 and $99,820 a year. Median annual earning of real estate brokers were $61,550 in offices of real estate agents and brokers and $44,920 in activities related to real estate.

Income usually increases as an agent gains experience, but individual motivation, economic conditions, and the type and location of the property also affect earnings. Sales workers who are active in community organizations and in local real estate associations can broaden their contacts and increase their earnings. A beginner's earnings often are irregular because a few weeks or even months may go by without a sale. Although some brokers allow an agent to draw against future earnings from a special account, the practice is not common with new employees. The beginner, therefore, should have enough money to live for about six months or until commissions increase.

The Downsides

In addition to lean income periods, sometimes a deal can fall through at the last minute. For example, buyers might be prequalified for a mortgage based on their income and amount of debt, but another financial examination is conducted just before closing. If the buyers have made another major purchase or been late in paying bills, or in some other way changed their financial picture, it can kill the deal.

Agents also have to be very careful when dealing with new clients who are strangers. This is especially true for women realtors. Brokers encourage their agents to work in pairs if possible and to always arrange the first meeting with the client to take place at the office, not at the property. Another precaution is not to take clients in your car, but to have them follow in their own cars.

Most every agent has experienced showing dozens of properties to a client without making a sale. While this is frustrating, it can be seen as an opportunity for an agent to gain additional knowledge about available properties.

Agents and brokers often work more than a standard forty-hour week. They usually work evenings and weekends and are always on call to suit the needs of clients. Business usually is slower during the winter season. Although the hours are long and frequently irregular, most agents and brokers have the freedom to determine their own schedules. Consequently, they can arrange their work so that they can have time off when they want it.

Travel Sales

Out of all the industries worldwide, travel and tourism continue to grow at an astounding rate. In fact, according to the Travel Works for America Council, the travel industry is the second largest employer in the United States after health services. Nearly everyone tries to take at least one vacation every year, and many people travel frequently on business. Some travel for education or for a special honeymoon or anniversary trip.

Constantly changing airfares and schedules, thousands of available vacation packages, and a vast amount of travel information on the Internet can make travel planning frustrating and time-consuming. To sort out the many travel options, tourists and businesspeople often turn to travel agents, who assess their needs and help them make the best possible travel arrangements. Also, many major cruise lines, resorts, and specialty travel groups use travel agents to promote their services to millions of people every year.

In general, travel agents give advice on destinations and make arrangements for transportation, hotel accommodations, car rentals, tours, and recreation. They may also advise on weather conditions, restaurants, and tourist attractions. For international travel, agents also provide information on customs regulations, required papers (passports, visas, and certificates of vaccination), and currency exchange rates.

Travel agents consult a variety of published and computer-based sources for information on departure and arrival times, fares, and hotel ratings and accommodations. They may visit hotels, resorts, and restaurants to evaluate comfort, cleanliness, and quality of food and service so that they can base recommendations on their own travel experiences or those of colleagues or clients.

Travel agents also promote their services, using telemarketing, direct mail, and the Internet. They make presentations to social and special-interest groups, arrange advertising displays, and suggest company-sponsored trips to business managers. Depending on the size of the travel agency, an agent may specialize by type of travel, such as leisure or business, or destination, such as Europe or Africa.

Travel agents spend most of their time behind a desk conferring with clients, completing paperwork, contacting airlines and hotels for travel arrangements, and promoting group tours. During vacation seasons and holiday periods, they may be under a great deal of pressure. Many agents, especially those who are self-employed, frequently work long hours. With advanced computer systems and telecommunication networks, some travel agents are able to work at home.

Training and Qualifications

The minimum requirement for working as a travel agent is a high school diploma or equivalent. Technology and computerization have increased the training needs, however, and many employers prefer applicants with more education, such as postsecondary vocational training.

Many vocational schools offer full-time travel agent programs that last several months, as well as evening and weekend programs. Travel agent courses also are offered in public adult education programs and in community and four-year colleges. A few colleges offer bachelor's or master's degrees in travel and tourism. Although few college courses relate directly to travel or tourism, a college education often shows employers an applicant's background in fields such as computer science, geography, communication, foreign languages, and world history. Courses in accounting and business management also are important, especially for those who expect to manage or start their own travel agencies.

The American Society of Travel Agents offers a correspondence course that provides a basic understanding of the travel industry. Travel agencies also provide on-the-job training for their employees, mainly in the form of computer instruction. All employers require computer skills of workers whose jobs involve the operation of airline and centralized reservations systems.

The abundance of travel information available through the Internet has resulted in a more informed customer who wants to deal with an expert when planning a trip. For this reason, continuing education is very important to the travel agent. Experienced agents can take advanced self-study or group-study courses from the Travel Institute, leading to the Certified Travel Counselor designation. The Travel Institute also offers marketing and sales skills development programs and destination specialist programs, which provide detailed knowledge of regions such as North America, Western Europe, the Caribbean, and the Pacific Rim. With the trend toward more specialization, these and other destination specialist courses are increasingly important.

Personal travel experience is an asset because knowledge about a city or foreign country often helps influence a client's travel plans. Patience and the ability to gain the confidence of clients also are useful qualities. Travel agents must be well-organized, accurate, and meticulous to compile information from various sources and plan and organize their clients' travel itineraries. Also, agents who specialize in business travel must work quickly and efficiently because business travel often must be arranged on short notice. In addition to computer skills, good writing and interpersonal and sales skills are important. Experience as an airline reservation agent can also be helpful.

Some employees start as reservation clerks or receptionists in travel agencies. With experience and some formal training, they can take on greater responsibilities and eventually assume travel agent duties. In agencies with many offices, travel agents may advance to office manager or to other managerial positions.

Those who start their own agencies generally have had experience in an established agency. Before they can receive commissions, these agents usually must gain formal approval from suppliers or corporations, such as airlines, cruise lines, or rail lines. For example, the Airlines Reporting Corporation and the International Airlines Travel Agency Network are the approving bodies for airlines. To gain approval, an agency must be financially sound and employ at least one experienced manager or travel agent.

There are no federal licensing requirements for travel agents, although in 2004 thirteen states required some form of registration or certification of retail sellers of travel services. More information may be obtained by contacting the Office of the Attorney General or Department of Commerce in each state.

Earnings for Travel Agents

Experience, sales ability, and the size and location of the agency determine the salary of a travel agent. Median annual earnings of travel agents were $27,640 in 2004. The middle 50 percent earned between $21,600 and $35,070. The lowest 10 percent earned less than $17,180, while the top 10 percent earned more than $44,090. Median earnings for travel agents employed in the travel arrangement and reservation services industry were $27,490.

Salaried agents usually enjoy standard employer-paid benefits that self-employed agents must provide for themselves. When traveling for personal reasons, agents usually get reduced rates for transportation and accommodations. In addition, agents sometimes take "familiarization" trips at low or no cost to themselves to learn about various vacation sites. These benefits attract many people to this occupation.

Earnings of travel agents who own their agencies depend primarily on commissions from travel-related bookings and service fees they charge clients. Often it takes time to acquire a sufficient number of clients to generate adequate earnings, so it is not unusual for new self-employed agents to have low earnings. Even established agents may experience reduced income during economic downturns.

The Downsides

According to many travel agents, the downside is that they seldom have enough free time to do all the traveling they would like to do. They are often tied to their desks, especially during peak travel periods such as the summer or important busy holidays. A newcomer would get to take at least one week a year, more once they've gained some seniority.

The work can also be frustrating at times. Customers might not always know what they want, or their plans can change, and, as a result, the travel agent might have to cancel or reroute destinations that had already been set. There are also times when things go wrong, such as airports closed by inclement weather or travelers becoming ill and needing to cancel reservations at the last minute.

Meet Some Sales Professionals

Perhaps the following accounts of three sales professionals will help you to decide whether this is the field for you. Read on to see what you think of working in sales.

Marty Gorelick, Sales Professional

Marty Gorelick has a bachelor of arts degree from Long Island University in Brooklyn, New York, and more than a dozen years of experience in computer hardware sales. He has attended seminars from all of the major computer manufacturers: Compaq, IBM, Hewlett Packard, Sony, Apple, and NEC. He is account manager for county government sales at GE Capital IT Solutions in Miami, Florida, where he services Metro-Dade, Broward, and Pasco Counties, plus all cities, towns, and villages within these areas.

"The computer industry is constantly changing," he says. "It is the fastest-growing industry in the world. Computers have made communications possible at lightning speed."

Marty cites advances in science, medicine, engineering, law, manufacturing, and education as just some examples of the ways in which computers have changed industry and society. All of these technological advances make his job that much more challenging.

"A typical day for me begins when I arrive at my office about 6:30 A.M.," Marty says. "After running the branch's allocation reports for all the salespeople in our office, I check my voice mail for any emergency issues that must be addressed quickly. An example might be a critical shipment that hasn't arrived on time or a file server that has developed a problem and is inoperable. These situations demand my immediate attention.

"I read my e-mail messages next. It's not unusual to have between five and fifteen messages ranging from company updates to manufacturer price changes to additions and deletions from any number of vendors. Some messages require a response ASAP; others can be addressed during the course of my regular day.

"Next stop is my in-box, which usually contains a collection of faxes that have arrived since I left the office at the end of business yesterday. These faxes could contain purchase orders, manufacturer promotional notices, seminar information, or news of a prospective customer looking for a great reseller like ours! All this, and the clock has not yet struck 8 A.M."

Once the official business day begins, Marty handles calls from customers concerning products, services, and orders. A typical day might include a quick staff meeting to discuss changes in plans or a new company procedure. Afternoons are usually spent finishing projects, faxing price quotes, and filing purchase orders and invoices.

In addition to the regular routine, Marty also puts out a special electronic price list every sixty days to reflect constantly changing prices. This process usually takes three to four working days. He also provides a manuscript of five thousand plus items from a third-party vendor. On any given day, he might also accompany a manufacturer to a client facility, where they call on any number of departments that have requested information or a demonstration of a new item.

"My day ends about the time that local traffic starts to build on the highway," Marty says. "This represents a ten-plus-hour day, five days a week, four-point-three weeks a month. To say this is a hectic day is putting it mildly. However, if you enjoy what you do, it can be and is a labor of love.

"The most enjoyable part of my position is helping my customers understand their needs in respect to the use of the equipment," Marty adds. "An example would be a customer interested in a laptop computer to do presentations at remote sites versus a client needing a laptop for communicating to his home base.

"The upside of my business is the satisfaction of being productive and helping others do the same. When I complete a project with confidence in a timely manner so my customers can enjoy productivity, I take a moment to sit back and breathe easy."

Marty also talks about the downsides of his career. "If I had to pick a project I least like to perform, it's the tons of paperwork that is a necessary evil in the day-to-day flow of business.

"The downside is always the fact of being in a race with the clock. I try never to let the clock win. I also refuse to let a discontinued product stop me from saying to a customer that I can't fill their needs. Somewhere out there is a replacement part. All salespeople are part detective. We look until we find what we need to help our customers."

Marty Gorelick offers some advice for anyone thinking about a career in computer sales. "For those who are considering entering my world, I would say to be prepared to plan for a very exciting career. Technology advances as fast as you can absorb yesterday's breakthroughs. Pick a school that offers the career path that you wish to follow (sales and marketing, computer network engineering, or service and repair). Attend as many seminars in the field as possible. Read as many journals that pertain to your area of interest. Spend as much time as you can afford talking to those around you in that particular field. Don't be afraid to roll up your sleeves and get your hands dirty. Ask a million questions. Experiment with the knowledge you've gained. Share your findings with others and always remember that, to achieve success, you must make learning a lifelong endeavor."

Donna Maas, Business Owner and Sales Professional

Donna Maas's formal studies include interior architecture, design, drafting, and oil painting. With a background in graphic art, she designs all marketing materials and packaging for MAAS Polishing Systemes of Willowbrook, Illinois. She serves as president and CEO of the company.

After six years of using various cleaning and polishing products and always wishing for something better, Maas asked a chemist to assist her in formulating a product that worked. The end result is MAAS Polishing Creme, a product that quickly restores all metals, fiberglass, Plexiglas, and oxidized paintwork to an unusually brilliant finish. "Little did I realize how this innovative formula would revolutionize the polishing products industry," she says.

"The job is glamorous, hectic, and unpredictable," Donna explains. "My role encompasses product development, designing marketing materials, and fielding calls from major retailers while maintaining balance in the offices, warehouse, and factory. This, combined with extensive traveling and television appearances on QVC to demonstrate my products, requires tremendous stamina. Everyone within the company, from my executive assistant to the shipping department, will tell you that every project I tackle must be treated with urgency, requiring immediate attention. This keeps my office personnel (including myself) operating at an unusually fast pace."

Hard work paid off for Donna. By her third year in business, she experienced an 800 percent growth on her initial investment. "It is tremendously fulfilling to obtain such rapid success and worldwide recognition," Donna says. "I would have to think long and hard if asked what the downside of my career is because I can't think of anything!"

Based on her experience, Donna Maas offers some advice for aspiring business owners. "I would advise others who wish to get into this field to stay focused. The most difficult thing for an entrepreneur to do is to focus. You have so many things coming at you all at once. I have learned to concentrate on the most promising opportunities. When you become scattered and attempt to address every opportunity, your success is hindered."

Jim LeClair, Business Owner and Sales Manager

Jim LeClair is the owner and sales manager of Advanced Computer Services in Lawrence, Kansas. He completed high school and took some secondary accounting and business classes. He also has attended ongoing seminars and classes that are offered by suppliers to enhance sales, technical training, and product knowledge.

"I was burned out on retail and on working for others," he says, "so my wife and I decided to form our own business. She had a strong computer background and I had more of the business background. We felt that our strengths would complement one another. Our company consists of training and network installations, network design to integration, support, and fiber optics, to name a few."

Jim's business employs five people who work Monday through Friday from 8 A.M. until 5 P.M. He strives to maintain a relaxed yet professional atmosphere, being mindful of employees' needs and working to keep morale as high as possible.

A typical day in Jim's business is difficult to describe, since things can change on short notice. Jim arrives at work at 7 A.M. and stays until 7 P.M. He spends about thirty percent of his time handling customers' needs, forty percent working on sales, and thirty percent on the daily activities involved in running the business.

Jim says, "What I like best is seeing how happy the customer is when we say, 'This is how the network will work,' and then the network performs as well or better than we anticipated. What I like least is having to discipline employees or contemplate lost sales.

"To be successful in this kind of work, it's very important to keep abreast of the current technology at all times, to be a good listener, to be flexible, to be able to read people, and to understand what they really want, not what they say they want. You have to be able to think quickly on your feet and have a semi-aggressive nature. You just can't take no for an answer. Still, you must sell the customers what they want. Don't try to sell people something that isn't right for them just because you can make some money."

Jim's advice to anyone interested in a similar career is based on basic personal traits. He says, "I'd advise those who are considering computer sales to be honest, to be fair, and always to do a good job. Our business has grown because we have gained the trust of both our customers and our employees."

For More Information

The following professional associations can provide additional information about each category of sales.

Retail Sales

Information on careers in retail sales may be obtained from the personnel offices of local stores, from state merchants' associations, or from local unions of the United Food and Commercial Workers International Union. Visit the website at www.ufcw.org.

In addition, general information about retailing is available from:

National Retail Federation
375 Seventh Street NW, Suite 1100
Washington, DC 20004
www.nrf.com

Services Sales

For details about employment opportunities for services sales representatives, contact employers who sell services in your area.

For information on careers and scholarships in hotel management and sales, contact:

The American Hotel & Lodging Association (AH&LA)
1201 New York Avenue NW, Suite 600
Washington, DC 20005
www.ahla.com

Manufacturing and Wholesale Sales

Information on manufacturers' agents is available from:

Sales & Marketing Executives International (SMEI)
PO Box 1390
Sumas, WA 98295
www.smei.org

Insurance Sales

General occupational information about insurance agents and brokers is available from the home office of many life and casualty insurance companies. Information on state licensing requirements may be obtained from the department of insurance in any state.

For information about insurance sales careers in independent agencies and brokerages, contact:

National Association of Professional Insurance Agents
400 North Washington Street
Alexandria, VA 22314
www.pianet.com

For information about professional designation programs for insurance sales, contact:

National Alliance for Insurance Education and Research
3630 North Hills Drive
Austin, TX 78731
www.scic.com

Chartered Property and Casualty Underwriters Society
   (CPCU)
720 Providence Road
Malvern, PA 19355
www.cpcusociety.org

Real Estate Sales

Details on licensing requirements for real estate agents, brokers, and appraisers are available from most local real estate and appraiser organizations or from the state real estate commission or board.

For more information about opportunities in real estate work, contact:

National Association of Realtors
30700 Russell Ranch Road
Westlake Village, CA 91362
www.realtor.com

Information on careers and licensing and certification requirements in real estate appraising is available from:

American Society of Appraisers (ASA)
555 Herndon Parkway, Suite 125
Herndon, VA 20170
www.appraisers.org

Appraisal Institute
550 West Van Buren Street, Suite 1000
Chicago, IL 60607
www.appraisalinstitute.org

Travel Sales

Information on sales careers in the travel industry can be obtained from:

American Society of Travel Agents (ASTA)
1101 King Street, Suite 200
Alexandria, VA 22314
www.astanet.com

Association of Retail Travel Agents (ARTA)
4320 North Miller Road
Scottsdale, AZ 85251
www.artaonline.com

The Travel Institute
148 Linden Street, Suite 305
Wellesley, MA 02482
www.thetravelinstitute.com

CHAPTER THREE

Careers in Marketing, Advertising, and Public Relations

Good times, bad times, there will always be advertising. In good times people want to advertise; in bad times they have to.
—Bruce Burton, *Town and Country*

Well before the sales team hits the road with its merchandise or services, another team of professionals—product developers and experts in marketing, advertising, public relations, and publicity—must perform its duties. The primary goal of marketing is to reach the consumer—to motivate or persuade a potential buyer; to sell a product, service, idea, or cause; to gain political support; or to influence public opinion.

The fundamental objective of any firm is to market its products or services profitably. To do so, an overall marketing policy must be established, including product development, market research, market strategies, sales approaches, advertising outlets, promotion possibilities, and effective pricing and packaging.

Marketing executives determine the demand for products and services offered by the firm and its competitors and identify potential consumers, such as business firms, wholesalers, retailers, government, or the general public. Mass markets are further categorized according to factors such as region, age, income, and lifestyle.

In small firms, all marketing responsibilities may be assumed by the owner or chief executive officer. In large firms, which may offer numerous products and services nationally or even globally, experienced professionals working together coordinate these and related activities.

Marketing

In simple terms, salespeople try to encourage others to buy what they are selling, and marketers try to figure out what consumers have a need for and how best to convey the message that the product meets that need. Marketers start at the beginning of the cycle and look at the customer, asking themselves, "I wonder what they need." Once that is determined, marketers look at their company and ask themselves, "Do we know how to produce it and can we make money doing it?"

The Marketing Process

Once marketers come up with a product idea—the ideas might come from talking to customers or as the result of brainstorming sessions—they start communicating with the product development department, which in some industries might consist of scientists or engineers. They form a team that includes marketing management, marketing researchers, engineers, advertisers, a financial advisor, and eventually salespeople.

First the team must decide if the product idea is something that customers really want, which involves conducting market research. Market researchers set up focus groups, bringing a group of consumers together and talking to them, finding out what isn't working in their present environment and what they truly need.

Professionals working in market research departments are tuned in to the consumer—what he or she worries about, desires, thinks, believes, and holds dear. Market researchers conduct surveys or one-on-one interviews, utilize existing research, test consumer reactions to new products or advertising copy, track sales figures and buying trends, and become overall experts on consumer behavior.

Agency research departments can design questionnaires or other methods of studying groups of people, implement the surveys, and interpret the results. Sometimes research departments hire an outside market research firm to handle this task. For example, a market researcher could come up with a procedure to test the public's reaction to a television commercial; the outside firm would put the procedure into action.

Marketing research assistants report directly to a research executive and are responsible for compiling and interpreting data and monitoring the progress of research projects. Once the market research is complete, marketers attempt to quantify that need in the marketplace. If thirty people have told them they need a particular device, that suggests a strong need, but the company can't afford to build something for just thirty people. It wants to make sure there are enough people out there who are willing to buy the product. This sparks another round of research to determine the target markets—those most likely to purchase the product—among all potential prospective buyers.

With successful research results, the concept development stage begins. This is the development of a word or paragraph that describes the product. In some instances, marketers then take that to engineers, who develop a prototype.

The prototype is taken to the marketplace for testing and evaluations. With feedback in hand, the team begins to make product improvements.

Once the marketers are at least 95 percent sure this is the product they—and the consumers—want, they give it a final test in the marketplace. They also test for claims. For example, a company might want to claim that its new hospital bed will prevent skin sores, but it needs to be able to document that claim.

If all test results point to being able to move forward, the engineers start figuring out how to mass produce the product, and marketers plan how the company can make money on it. For that, they have to look at the production cost and how much customers would be willing to pay for it. A misconception in this area is that a profit percentage is simply added to the production cost, resulting in the selling price. In reality, prices are not determined that way; they are determined by what people are willing to pay. If that price doesn't allow for a resonable profit margin based on the production costs, the product may not make it past the planning phase.

If a product's price is deemed profitable, the next step is promotion planning. Now that the company has a product, it has to find a way to get the word out. The appropriate team members make brochures and design advertising. At the same time, production schedules are set up. Marketing experts need to know how fast the product can be made, how quickly it can be offered to the public, how many will be bought, and how large the profit will be.

Once a date is set for introducing the product, the sales force is brought in and taught how to present it. Then the product is monitored to see if it is meeting sales projections. If it is not, management wants to know why and what is going to be done about it. Often, though, if it is meeting or exceeding expectations, management still wants to know why. That's the way it goes in a competitive business.

Job Settings for Marketing Professionals

Marketing professionals are found in virtually every industry, including motor vehicle dealers, printing and publishing firms, department stores, computer and data processing services firms, management and public relations firms, and advertising agencies.

Because marketers and advertising professionals work hand in hand, many marketing departments are located within corporate advertising departments or private advertising agencies. Marketing firms function similarly to advertising agencies and work toward the same goals—identifying and targeting specific audiences that will be receptive to specific products, services, or ideas.

The Downsides

Although marketing is considered by many to be a step up from sales, it does have a downside. If the company is not making the expected profit, marketers could easily lose their jobs. Their responsibilities for sales volume and profit are the same as those that salespeople must meet.

In essence, marketers make an agreement with sales departments and personnel. For example, they might decide, "OK, we are going to sell a hundred units of product X to a particular customer." But if too much money is spent in product development or advertising and only ninety units are sold, although the salesperson has the first responsibility, the marketing team is also responsible. Marketing had agreed on what could be sold on specific advertising and on setting a certain price. If the mark is missed, it's the marketers' jobs that are also on the line.

Another downside is that marketers usually supervise salespeople, but the sales force often makes more money than the marketers do—possibly a lot more money. To make up for the discrepancy, marketers usually also receive a good pension plan and bonuses.

Marketers work long hours, often including evenings and weekends. Working under pressure is unavoidable as schedules change, problems arise, and deadlines and goals must be met.

Training and Qualifications

A wide range of educational backgrounds is suitable for entry into marketing jobs, but many employers prefer those with experience in related occupations plus a broad liberal arts background. A bachelor's degree in sociology, psychology, literature, journalism, or philosophy, among other subjects, is acceptable. However, requirements vary, depending upon the particular job.

Some employers prefer a bachelor's or master's degree in business administration with an emphasis on marketing. Courses in business law, economics, accounting, finance, mathematics, and statistics are advantageous. In highly technical industries, such as computer and electronics manufacturing, a bachelor's degree in engineering or science, combined with a master's degree in business administration, is preferred.

Courses in management and completion of an internship while in school are highly recommended. Experts advise beginning your job search before you near graduation. Those who arrange internships have an edge; they've already become familiar faces on the job. When an opening comes up, a known commodity—someone who performed well during the internship—is likely to be chosen over an unknown one. Learn as much as you can about the agency or firm you're interested in. In other words, target your prospects.

Familiarity with word processing and database applications also is important for many positions. Computer skills are vital because marketing, product promotion, and advertising on the Internet are increasingly common. The ability to communicate in a foreign language may enhance employment opportunities in many rapidly growing areas around the country, especially in cities with large Spanish-speaking populations.

Those interested in becoming marketing managers should be mature, creative, highly motivated, resistant to stress, flexible, and decisive. The ability to communicate persuasively, both orally and in writing, with other managers, staff members, and the public is essential. These managers also need tact, good judgment, and exceptional ability to establish and maintain effective personal relationships with supervisory and professional staff members and client firms.

Getting Ahead

Because of the importance and high visibility of their jobs, marketing managers often are prime candidates for advancement to the highest ranks. Well-trained, experienced, successful managers may be promoted to higher positions in their own, or other, firms. Some become top executives. Marketing managers with extensive experience and sufficient capital even open their own businesses.

Most marketing management positions are filled by promoting experienced staff or related professional personnel. For example, many managers are former sales representatives, purchasing agents, or buyers, or they might have worked as product, advertising, promotions, or public relations specialists. In small firms with a limited number of positions, advancement to a management position usually comes slowly. Promotion may occur more quickly in larger firms.

Although experience, ability, and leadership are emphasized for promotion, advancement can be accelerated by participation in management training programs conducted by many large firms. Many firms also provide their employees with continuing education opportunities, either in-house or at local colleges and universities, and encourage employee participation in seminars and conferences, often provided by professional societies.

Several marketing and related associations sponsor national or local management training programs in collaboration with colleges and universities. Course subjects include brand and product management, international marketing, sales management evaluation, telemarketing and direct sales, interactive marketing, promotion, marketing communication, market research, organizational communication, and data processing systems procedures and management. Many firms pay all or part of the cost for those who successfully complete courses. .

Some associations offer certification programs for these managers. As a sign of competence and achievement in the field of marketing, certification is particularly important in a competitive job market. For example, Sales & Marketing Executives International offers a management certification program based on education and job performance.

Earnings for Marketing Professionals

According to a survey by the National Association of Colleges and Employers, starting salaries for marketing majors graduating in 2005 averaged $33,873. Salary levels vary substantially, depending on the level of managerial responsibility, length of service, education, size of firm, location, and industry. For example, manufacturing firms usually pay these managers higher salaries than do nonmanufacturing firms. For sales managers, the size of the sales territory is another important determinant of salary. Many managers earn bonuses equal to 10 percent or more of their salaries.

Median annual earnings for marketing managers were $87,640 in 2004. In the areas employing the largest numbers of marketing managers, average salaries in 2004 were as follows:

Computer systems design and related services	$107,030
Management of companies and enterprises	$98,700
Insurance carriers	$86,810
Architectural, engineering, and related services	$83,610
Depository credit intermediation	$76,450

Advertising

"What's in your wallet?" "Don't leave home without it." "Can you hear me now?" Such phrases are familiar to most of us because of the effective work of advertising specialists. Some consider this phenomenon a nuisance that interrupts television programming and encourages people to buy products that they may or may not really need. Others look upon it as a great public service. A dominating force in our society, mass-media advertising is a multimillion-dollar industry dating back to the invention of movable type in the mid-1400s.

Advertising Agencies

Virtually every type of business makes use of advertising in some form, often through the services of an advertising agency. Companies often look to advertising as a way of boosting sales by increasing the public's exposure to a product.

Most companies do not have staff with the necessary skills or experience to create effective advertisements. In addition, many advertising campaigns are temporary, so employers would have difficulty maintaining their own advertising staff. Instead, companies commonly solicit bids from ad agencies to develop advertising for them. Next, ad agencies offering their services to the company often make presentations. The real work for ad agencies begins when they win an account. Various departments within an agency, such as creative, production, media, and research, work together to meet the client's goal of increasing sales.

There are more than fifty thousand advertising and public relations services establishments in the United States. About four out of ten write copy and prepare artwork, graphics, and other creative work, and then place the resulting ads on television, radio, and the Internet or in periodicals, newspapers, and other advertising media. Within the industry, only these full-service establishments are known as advertising agencies. Many of the largest agencies are international, with a substantial proportion of their revenue coming from abroad.

Most advertising firms specialize in a particular market niche. Some companies produce and solicit outdoor advertising, such as billboards and electric displays. Others place ads in buses, subways, taxis, airports, and bus terminals. A small number of firms produce aerial advertising, while others distribute circulars, handbills, and free samples.

Groups within agencies have been created to serve their clients' electronic advertising needs on the Internet. Online advertisements link users from one website to a company's or product's website, where information such as new product announcements, contests, and product catalogs appears, and from which purchases may be made.

Some firms are not involved in the creation of ads at all; instead, they sell advertising time or space on radio and television stations or in publications. Because these firms do not produce advertising, their staffs are mostly sales workers.

The work at an advertising agency is often divided among several individuals or departments, usually including the following:

- **Account executives** make sure that work is completed satisfactorily and on time and to the client's satisfaction. Account executives must be savvy about their agencies and aware of each client's desires and needs. Their responsibilities lie more in the business arena than in the creative aspects of the business.
- **Art directors** must be able to effectively present a theme or idea in convincing visual form through text, illustration, color, photography, or cinematography.
- **Creative directors** supervise all employees and oversee all activities in the agency. At the top of the hierarchy, creative directors must, of course, be creative as well as possess people skills and solid business acumen.
- **Researchers** seek to determine what kind of audience would be interested in a particular product or service, why they are interested in the product, and how the public is reacting to advertising campaigns already in place.
- **Media people** ensure that commercials are aired on radio and television and that advertisements get into magazines and newspapers.

Other advertising positions include television producers, print production managers, graphic artists, illustrators, photographers, copywriters, freelance writers, print production personnel, and traffic managers.

Advertising Copywriters

Advertising copywriters are the real creative force behind ad campaigns. They are the ones who dream up the words for commercials and advertisements and conjure the themes for advertising campaigns. Copywriters may also be responsible for creating articles about products or services, sales promotion materials, public relations items, billboards, and promotional brochures. Copywriters usually begin their work by meeting with the client and/or account executive. After gathering as much information as possible, they let their imaginations flow while looking for a slant on why a product or service is different from all others of its kind. Then they proceed to develop a new advertising campaign with their innovative ideas.

Advertising Sales Agents

Advertising sales agents, also called account executives or advertising sales representatives, sell or solicit advertising, including graphic art, advertising space in publications, custom-made signs, or television and radio advertising time. More than half of all advertising sales agents work in the information sector, mostly for media firms, including television and radio broadcasters, print and Internet publishers, and cable program distributors. Other agents work for firms engaged in direct mail advertising or display and outdoor advertising, such as billboards and signs. Because most revenue for magazines, newspapers, directories, and broadcasters is generated from advertising, sales agents play an important role in their success.

Outside sales agents call on clients and prospects. They may have an appointment, or they may make cold calls, arriving without prior arrangement. Inside sales agents work on the employer's premises and handle sales to customers who walk in or telephone the firm to inquire about advertising. Some also may make telephone sales calls—calling prospects, attempting to sell the media firm's advertising space or time, and arranging follow-up appointments between interested prospects and outside sales agents.

Within the advertising industry, media representative firms sell advertising space or time for media owners, including print and Internet publishers, radio and television stations, and cable systems. These firms maintain offices in major cities and employ their own teams of advertising sales agents. The agents they employ work exclusively with the executives at advertising agencies, called media buyers, who purchase advertising space for their clients. Media representative firms may represent any number of publications and radio or television stations, selling space or time to advertising agencies with clients who want to initiate a national advertising campaign or place advertisements outside their local markets.

Sales agents are employed by local publications or radio and television stations and are responsible for sales in a local territory. Obtaining new accounts is an important part of the job for these agents, who may spend much of their time traveling to and visiting prospective advertisers and current clients. During a sales call, they discuss the client's advertising needs and suggest how their products and services can meet those needs.

During the first meeting with a client, sales agents gather background information and explain how specific types of advertising will help promote a client's products or services most effectively. Next, the agent prepares an advertising proposal to present to the client. This entails determining the advertising medium to be used, preparing sample advertisements, and providing clients with estimates of the cost of the proposal. Consolidation in the media industries has brought the sale of different types of advertising under one roof. Sales are increasingly made of integrated packages that include advertisements to be placed in print, online, and with a broadcast subsidiary.

After a contract has been established, advertising sales agents serve as the main contact between the client and the firm. They handle communication between the parties and assist the client in developing sample artwork or radio and television spots. They also arrange for commercial taping sessions and may accompany clients to the sessions.

Beyond selling, advertising sales agents have other duties as well. They analyze sales statistics, prepare reports, and handle the scheduling of their appointments and work hours. They read about new and existing products and monitor the sales, prices, and products of their competitors. In many firms, the advertising sales agent handles the drafting of contracts specifying the advertising work to be performed and its cost, as well as the billing and record keeping for their customers' accounts, which may include customer service responsibilities such as answering questions or addressing any problems the client may have with the proposal. Sales agents also are responsible for developing sales tools, promotional plans, and media kits that they use to help make the sale.

Training and Qualifications

Most employers expect applicants to have college degrees. For those who aspire to become account executives, an M.B.A. is especially important. Many schools offer programs in advertising, and a number of top advertising agencies offer in-house training programs for copywriters and account managers.

Since copywriters deal with a wide cross section of ideas and concepts, a general liberal arts background in combination with business is particularly valued. Courses in such subjects as economics, history, journalism, marketing, advertising, math, social sciences, speech, literature, business administration, human relations, and creative writing are recommended.

Copywriters need the skills that all writers should have—the ability to produce clear, concise prose. Therefore, writing experience in the form of published articles; participation in school, church, or yearbook publications; work for local newspapers or radio or television studios; and internships are all worthwhile endeavors.

Candidates should prepare a portfolio containing at least three ads from previous advertising campaigns. These can be class assignments or real ads from actual clients. If you have no advertising experience at all, present potential employers with samples of your published writing.

For advertising sales agents, some employers prefer applicants with a college degree, particularly for sales positions that require meeting with clients. Courses in marketing, leadership, communication, business, and advertising are helpful. For those who sell over the telephone or who have a proven record of successfully selling other products, a high school diploma may be sufficient. After gaining entry into the occupation, successful sales experience becomes more important than education when looking for a position. In general, smaller companies are more willing to hire unproven individuals.

Because they represent their employers to the executives of client organizations, advertising sales agents must have excellent interpersonal and written communication skills. Employers look for applicants who possess a pleasant personality, are honest and trustworthy, and present a neat professional appearance. Self-motivation, organization, persistence, independence, and the ability to multitask are required because advertising sales agents set their own schedules and perform their duties without much supervision.

Training takes place mainly on the job. In most cases, an experienced sales manager instructs a newly hired advertising sales agent who lacks sales experience. Advancement means taking on bigger, more important clients. Agents with proven leadership ability and a strong sales record may advance to supervisory and managerial positions such as sales supervisor, sales manager, or vice president of sales. Frequent contact with managers of other departments and people in other firms provides sales agents with leads about job openings, enhancing advancement opportunities. In small firms, where the number of supervisory and management positions is limited, advancement may come slowly. Promotion may occur more quickly in large firms.

Earnings for Advertising Specialists

There is a considerable range of salaries in this field, particularly in different regions of the country. The median annual salary in advertising agencies is about $33,000. Junior copywriters may start out in the low twenties; writers with senior status may earn

$60,000 to $100,000 and even more as creative directors. Median annual earnings were $63,610 for advertising and promotions managers in 2004.

Most advertising sales workers are paid a combination of salaries, commissions, and bonuses. Commissions are usually based on the amount of sales, whereas bonuses may depend on individual performance, on the performance of all sales workers in the group or district, or on the company's overall performance. Median annual earnings in 2004 for all advertising sales agents were $40,300, including commissions. The industries hiring the largest numbers of agents are advertising and related services; radio and television broadcasting; and newspaper, periodical, book, and directory publishers.

In addition to their earnings, advertising sales agents usually are reimbursed for business expenses, such as transportation costs, meals, hotels, and entertaining customers. They often receive benefits, such as health and life insurance, pension plans, vacation and sick leave, personal use of a company car, and frequent flier mileage. Some companies offer incentives, such as free vacation trips or gifts for outstanding sales workers.

The larger the agency or account, the higher the salary will be. The best locations for jobs are in large cities, such as New York, Chicago, Detroit, Boston, Atlanta, Dallas, Minneapolis, and Los Angeles.

Public Relations

You might be surprised to learn that the concept of public relations is definitely not a new invention. It dates back to 1787, during the time of the Constitutional Convention. And in the 1800s, both the North and the South made use of the media during the Civil War in an attempt to persuade the populace to adopt their way of thinking.

The goal of public relations remains the same—to sway the public in a particular direction or to build, maintain, and promote positive relationships between two factions: the agencies (or companies) and the public.

An organization's reputation, profitability, and even its continued existence can depend on the degree to which its targeted "publics" support its goals and policies. Public relations specialists, also referred to as communications specialists and media specialists, serve as advocates for businesses, nonprofit associations, universities, hospitals, and other organizations to build and maintain positive relationships with the public. As managers recognize the growing importance of good public relations to the success of their organizations, they increasingly rely on public relations specialists for advice on the strategy and policy of such programs.

Informing the general public, interest groups, and stockholders of an organization's policies, activities, and accomplishments is an important part of a public relations specialist's job. The work also involves keeping management aware of public attitudes and the concerns of the many groups and organizations with which they must deal.

The work of a public relations practitioner falls into six main categories:

1. **Research.** This includes all of the preliminary work that is undertaken to determine the client's goals so that a plan to achieve them can be devised. Library and Internet research, client interviews, surveys, opinion polls, and collecting data are all part of this.
2. **Program work.** Once research is completed, a plan is set up based upon the findings.
3. **Writing and editing.** This may include press releases, presentations to clients, internal memos, reports, and magazine articles.
4. **Special events.** Included in this category are press conferences, special appearances, and autograph signings. All are carefully orchestrated to gain the greatest amount of attention.

5. **Media placement.** It is important to select the most important information to release, choose a good time to release it, and send it to the most advantageous receivers.
6. **Fund-raising.** Fund-raising is what sustains nonprofit organizations. Possible events include membership drives, direct solicitation, and benefit banquets.

Those who work as generalists in the field must be able to perform a wide range of duties at the same time. In any given week, they may write press releases for one client, design a brochure for another, approach an editor for a third, meet with a talk show host for a fourth, implement a promotion for a fifth, set up a press conference for a sixth, put together a press kit for a seventh, work out the beginnings of a client contract for an eighth, and field media questions for a ninth.

In the government arena, public relations specialists may be called press secretaries, communications specialists, or information officers. A senator's press secretary informs the elected official's constituents of his or her accomplishments and responds to questions from the media and the press. The press secretary schedules and appears at press conferences and issues statements from his or her superior.

Training and Qualifications

There are no defined standards for entry into a public relations career. A college degree combined with public relations experience, usually gained through an internship, is considered excellent preparation for public relations work; in fact, internships are becoming vital to obtaining employment. The ability to communicate effectively is essential. Many entry-level public relations specialists have a college major in public relations, journalism, advertising, or communication.

Some firms seek college graduates who have worked in electronic or print journalism. Other employers seek applicants with demonstrated communication skills and training or experience in a field related to the firm's business—information technology, health, science, engineering, sales, or finance, for example.

Many colleges and universities offer bachelor's and postsecondary degrees in public relations, usually in a journalism or communications department. In addition, many other colleges offer at least one course in this field. A common public relations sequence includes courses in public relations principles and techniques; public relations management and administration, including organizational development; writing, emphasizing news releases, proposals, annual reports, scripts, speeches, and related items; visual communications, including desktop publishing and computer graphics; and research, emphasizing social science research and survey design and implementation. Specialties are offered in public relations for business, government, and nonprofit organizations. Courses in advertising, journalism, business administration, finance, political science, psychology, sociology, and creative writing also are helpful.

Many colleges help students gain part-time internships in public relations that provide valuable experience and training. The U.S. Armed Forces also can be an excellent place to gain training and experience. Membership in local chapters of the Public Relations Student Society of America (affiliated with the Public Relations Society of America) or the International Association of Business Communicators provides an opportunity for students to exchange views with public relations specialists and to make professional contacts that may help them find a job in the field. A portfolio of published articles, television or radio programs, slide presentations, and other work is an asset in finding a job. Writing for a school publication or television or radio station provides valuable experience and material for one's portfolio.

Creativity, initiative, good judgment, and the ability to express thoughts clearly and simply are essential skills. Decision-making, problem-solving, and research skills also are important. People who choose public relations as a career need an outgoing personality, self-confidence, an understanding of human psychology, and an enthusiasm for motivating people. They should be competitive yet able to function as part of a team and open to new ideas.

Some organizations, particularly those with large public relations staffs, have formal training programs for new employees. In smaller companies, new employees work under the guidance of experienced staff members. Beginners are often assigned to maintaining files of material about company activities, scanning newspapers and magazines for relevant articles to clip, and assembling information for speeches and pamphlets. They also may answer calls from the press and public, work on invitation lists and details for press conferences, or escort visitors and clients. After gaining experience, they may begin to write news releases, speeches, and articles for publication or design and carry out public relations programs. Public relations specialists in smaller firms usually get all-around experience, whereas those in larger firms tend to be more specialized.

Promotion to supervisory jobs may come as public relations specialists show that they can handle more demanding assignments. In public relations firms, a beginner might be hired as a research assistant or account coordinator and be promoted to account executive, senior account executive, account manager, and, eventually, vice president. A similar career path is followed in corporate public relations, although the titles may differ. Some experienced public relations specialists start their own consulting firms.

The Public Relations Society of America accredits public relations specialists who have at least five years of experience in the field and have passed a comprehensive six-hour examination (five hours written, one hour oral). The International Association of Business Communicators also has an accreditation program for professionals in the communication field, including public relations specialists. Those who meet all the requirements of the program earn the Accredited Business Communicator (ABC) designation. Candidates must have at least five years of experience in a communication field and pass a written and oral examination.

They also must submit a portfolio of work samples demonstrating involvement in a range of communication projects and a thorough understanding of communication planning.

Employers may consider professional recognition through accreditation a sign of competence in this field, which could be especially helpful in a competitive job market.

Earnings for Public Relations Personnel

Median annual earnings for salaried public relations specialists were $43,830 in 2004. The middle 50 percent earned between $32,970 and $59,360; the lowest 10 percent earned less than $25,750, and the top 10 percent earned more than $81,120. Median annual earnings in the industries employing the largest numbers of public relations specialists were as follows:

Advertising and related services	$50,450
Management of companies and enterprises	$47,330
Business, professional, labor, political, and similar organizations	$45,400
Local government	$44,550
Colleges, universities, and professional schools	$39,610

Meet Some Professionals

Read the following accounts of professionals working in marketing, advertising, and public relations to see whether one of these careers might be right for you.

Edward Pitkoff, Marketing and Advertising Professional

Edward Pitkoff of Omaha, Nebraska, attended the Philadelphia Museum School of Art, the Pennsylvania Academy of Fine Arts, Temple University, and Studio School of Art and Design, all in Philadelphia. He also attended a wide variety of marketing and advertising seminars and the School of Visual Arts in New York for a course in television production and direction. He has held several high-ranking positions in marketing, advertising, and sales and is founder and president of Creative Decisions, Inc., of New York.

"My career began in 1961," says Edward. "After twelve years in positions of designer, assistant art director, art director, and creative director, a freelance business presented itself and I formed Ed Pitkoff Studios, which expanded and evolved into Creative Decisions, Inc., in 1973, and there the story truly started."

Edward was attracted to the idea of producing high-quality creative advertising that could persuade a consumer to purchase a product. He credits a mentor who taught him "to marry the communication to the consumer so that the buyer could visualize themselves as part of the product."

Edward Pitkoff's advice to those interested in this field involves focus. "Don't ever become distracted," he says. "Always keep your focus on the business of advertising. And remember, what you might want to say to sell this product or service really isn't important. The only thing that is important is what would be compelling to the consumers. What do they want to hear? What do they want to buy? Ultimately, it is the consumers who judge how well your message has come across. If the product sells, then you know your focused communication has reached its audience."

Dennis Abelson, Marketing and Advertising Professional

Dennis Abelson earned a bachelor of arts degree in classical languages from Washington University in St. Louis, Missouri, and a master of science in journalism degree in advertising from Northwestern University's Medill School of Communications in Evanston, Illinois. He has experience as a copywriter, associate creative director, and creative director.

Dennis was working as a freelance writer but grew tired of the isolation and wanted more lucrative creative challenges. He was approached by someone who had seen one of his promotional mailings, and together they started a full-service marketing, consulting, and communications firm. After a slow start, the company began to grow and become more successful. Dennis and his partner ultimately established their corporate identity as Matrix Partners.

The company provides services such as packaging, advertising, promotion, direct mail, and sales presentations. Their clients include a distributor of computer cabling and networking systems, an agricultural biotechnology company, a manufacturer of diving equipment, and several food vendors.

"I originally got into the creative end of advertising because I couldn't see myself holding down a nine-to-five job," Dennis says. "It also gave me the opportunity to keep pursuing my interests in audio engineering and cartooning. In my undergraduate years, I was program director of the campus radio station as well as the creator of a weekly comic strip in the campus paper.

While Dennis says that there is not a typical day in his business, an average day might begin at 8 A.M. and include these duties: revising ad copy, attending project-status meetings, finalizing ad copy and sending it to the client, reviewing logo designs for a new account, performing an online trademark search for a proposed line, eating lunch while working on a presentation, taking calls from clients, working with designers and writers on projects, editing presentations, and writing a direct mailer. In Dennis's estimation, this day would end at about 11 P.M.

"What does it mean to be doing my kind of work?" asks Dennis. "At times it seems totally thankless, but in what other profession do you get paid to legally hallucinate, to play creatively with concepts and pictures?"

Among the upsides of his work, Dennis lists a lack of corporate politics or hidden agendas, the opportunity to gain knowledge about many different industries, and the satisfaction of contributing to the success of a client's business. On the other hand, the downsides include the long hours, difficult clients, and logistical and budgetary constraints on creativity.

Dennis Abelson offers this advice about his career: "I would tell others who are considering a career in advertising and marketing to start with the largest organization that will hire you. And be prepared for the long haul."

Tracy Larrua, Senior Account Executive

Tracy Larrua has more than twenty years of experience in public relations, marketing, and advertising. She attended a performing arts high school, then entered business college but ended up working at an advertising agency instead of getting her degree. She quickly worked her way up the ladder in advertising after six years as an account executive with Ogilvy and Mather. She then began working in public relations, where she has stayed ever since.

In her native Hawaii, Tracy was the owner of TL Promotes before relocating to Los Angeles in 1992. She is active in the culinary, visual, and music arts arenas, and she currently represents musicians, artists, and a production company.

"My typical day is spent writing pitch letters, developing story ideas for editors, and adding, deleting, and updating our media database to be as up-to-date as possible as to what is going on with our clients," says Tracy. "While wearing a headset, I also make a lot of phone calls. The atmosphere is never relaxed. Actually, it is usually very high stress, but it's a fun stress. Our typical work week is forty-plus hours, but depending on client demand, workload, and editorial deadlines, it can easily turn into a sixty-plus week."

Tracy has some advice for anyone interested in a career in public relations. "I would recommend that others who are interested in entering this profession get in on the ground floor and act like a sponge. Soak up everything you can," she stresses. "As you start developing your skills, you'll find yourself ascending. Also, stay flexible. This industry has gone through all sorts of changes. Learn, adapt, and adopt a fearless attitude."

Tracy also adds a word of caution. "If you aren't the 'people type,' don't even consider getting into this business. You have to be comfortable and persuasive in talking to people—all kinds of people. Remember, your personality skills count for a lot in this industry."

Betsy Nichol, Public Relations Business Owner

Betsy Nichol heads her own public relations agency, Nichol & Company of New York. She earned a bachelor of science degree in journalism from Boston University and has continued to enhance her credentials through seminars and professional workshops.

Like many public relations specialists, Betsy began her career as a journalist. She served a three-month internship at Fairchild Publications and ultimately held a full-time position at its publication, *Home Furnishings Daily*. After three years, Betsy was recruited by a small public relations firm.

"Early on in my career," Betsy says, "someone told me I should have my own business, and at the time I thought he was crazy, but as the years went by, I realized that I'm one of those people who is better at being my own boss than working for someone else."

Betsy's initial attraction to the field of public relations was its fast pace and varied responsibilities. She was interested in meeting people from different professions and having the opportunity to learn about many different subjects.

"I also like to communicate in writing," says Betsy, "and good writing skills are essential in the PR business. There's never a dull moment in this business, and being successful requires many of the same skills as being a journalist. It's been an exciting journey.

"Being head of a public relations firm is very hectic," Nichol stresses. "The phone is always ringing, and you never know if it's a client with a crisis, an editor on a deadline, or an employee with a question."

As head of the agency, Betsy spends a good deal of time in meetings with clients or consulting with them by telephone. She also meets with employees to discuss their progress on various projects. In addition, she attends to new business, keeps up with industry standards, and monitors her company accordingly. To accomplish all of this, Betsy continually monitors her e-mail, talks on the phone, gives instructions to staff, and responds to faxes, notes, and mail that require her attention.

Networking is also an important part of Betsy's career. She attends and speaks at many meetings, workshops, and other events that can lead to new business, provide insight into industry trends, and form alliances that enable her to better serve her clients.

Betsy talks about the ups and downs of her profession. "The public relations business offers endless ways to express one's creativity. It also demands that one think strategically to help clients solve their problems, which keeps me on my toes and makes every day action packed.

"In running a business of twelve people, there is also a great sense of teamwork and caring among the staffers—not a typical office environment. The interaction between us produces exciting results and great fun. The downside is that we often have to cancel evening plans and work late to meet breaking deadlines."

Betsy Nichol offers a suggestion to those interested in public relations. "My advice to others who are considering this field is to work hard and be flexible and both patient and impatient in your quest for success."

Joanne Levine, Public Relations Professional and Business Owner

Joanne Levine owns Chicago-based Lekas & Levine Public Relations, Inc., which specializes in pursuing media publicity for small and mid-sized businesses.

Joanne did not enter the field in the usual way. She majored in English in college but had no ambition to focus on public relations. She joined local community groups while raising her children, and this became a stepping-stone to her future career. While organizing a fund-raiser for one of the organizations, Joanne worked with a public relations professional on the publicity committee. She learned a lot from the experience and became fascinated by the work.

"At the same time, my very creative brother was writing music, forming bands, and starting wacky side businesses," Joanne says. "One of his companies created and marketed original adult board games he designed. To test my newfound skills, each time he introduced a game, I sent out press releases to the media. The first game, Danger Island, even included me as one of the characters. When the reporters arrived, I became part of the story. We got spectacular local and national coverage.

"That first project really whetted my appetite. From there, I began publicizing my husband's retail stores, more civic groups, and the like. One day, I thought about the fact that I was doing a great job and not getting paid for it. I recruited my brother's wife to help me, and we wrote a press release about two sisters-in-law who started a public relations company devoted to small businesses. We got an immediate response from the local chain of newspapers. They wrote a feature article about our company, even though we had no clients. The rest, they say, is history. From that initial article, the phone began to ring, and within a month or two, we had five clients. It's been word of mouth ever since."

Joanne describes media public relations as popular among clients but stressful for the PR professional. In addition to writing copy for brochures and planning special events, Joanne estimates that eighty percent of her time is spent helping her clients to appear in newspapers, magazines, and trade publications, as well as on television and radio. Media publicity increases a client's visibility and adds credibility to a client's reputation.

Despite the appeal of media publicity to clients, it is not as popular among the public relations professionals who must do the work. As Joanne says, "With an ad, you know what day it will appear, what size it will be, and exactly what it will say. With an article, I hold my breath until the client and I read it in the publication. With a taped interview on radio or television, I wait to see if anything was cut or taken out of context. While my press release and phone conversation with an editor might have been chock-full of the kind of information I hope they will relay to the public, there are no guarantees such as those in advertising. I work with editors and writers who are always on deadline, always over-worked, but nevertheless always looking for a good angle. For these reasons, my job can be stressful and sometimes plagued with problems that are completely out of my control."

Despite the pressure, Joanne finds that the positive aspects of her work outweigh the negative. "When all goes well, there's noth-ing like it," she says. "I have seen the positive results of good, steady media campaigns time and time again. And more than once in a while, a really big media appearance can make an overnight dif-ference in someone's business. The client is on cloud nine, his or her phones begin to ring off the hook with new business, and I am showered with praise and gratitude. I often get to know my clients well and enjoy friendly, upbeat working relationships with them. The knowledge that I am helping to make a client's business grow is very rewarding."

Based on her experience, Joanne Levine offers some practical advice for aspiring public relations specialists. "If you want a career in media publicity, I would advise you to read, read, read," she says. "Study the format of newspapers, watch the twelve, five, six, and ten o'clock news. Read every magazine you can get your hands on and note how things are laid out. Reporters have certain 'beats,' and if you can zero in on what they write about, half the battle is won. Familiarizing oneself with the media is a never-ending responsibility. While there are a few good media guides that provide information, this is not a substitute for studying the style of an individual person, section, or publication. Also, as the media faces the same cutbacks and consolidations as any other industry, frequent changes in personnel happen at a rapid pace.

"If you don't want to go through the trial-and-error process as much as I did, try to get an internship with a PR company. I have used graduate students from the Medill School of Journalism at

Northwestern University as freelancers several times. Just remember that in order to make it in this field, you need a good imagination and the ability to find an 'angle.'

"I can't tell you how many times a client has said, 'I do a better job than anyone else in town and I truly care about my customers.' That's very nice, but it's boring! Find out why the client does a better job. What does he or she do differently? Is the business owner an interesting person? What are his or her hobbies? The list goes on and on. You must be able to pick someone's brain until something newsworthy pops out. Then, you must learn who might be fascinated with your information, so much so that they want to inform their readers about it or share it with their television audience."

For More Information

The following professional associations can aid in your job search. Many of the publications these organizations produce are available in public libraries.

The American Marketing Association is a professional society of marketing and market research executives, sales and promotion managers, advertising specialists, academics, and others interested in marketing. It fosters research; sponsors seminars, conferences, and student marketing clubs; and provides a placement service. It also offers a certification program for marketing managers. The organization publishes the *Journal of Marketing, Journal of Marketing Research, Journal of Health Care Marketing*, and an international membership directory. For more information, write to:

American Marketing Association
311 South Wacker Drive, Suite 5800
Chicago, IL 60606
www.marketingpower.com

Members of the National Council for Marketing and Public Relations are communications specialists working within community, technical, and junior colleges in areas including alumni, community, government, media, and public relations as well as marketing, publications, and special events. The association works to foster improved relations between two-year colleges and their communities throughout the United States and Canada. The association holds an annual conference with exhibits, national surveys, and needs assessments and publishes a journal called *Counsel*. Additional information can be obtained by contacting:

National Council for Marketing and Public Relations
PO Box 336039
Greeley, CO 80633
www.ncmpr.org

Sales & Marketing Executives International offers a management certification program. Write to:

Sales & Marketing Executives International (SMEI)
PO Box 1390
Sumas, WA 98295
www.smei.org

For information about career opportunities in public relations, contact:

Public Relations Society of America (PRSA)
33 Maiden Lane, Eleventh Floor
New York, NY 10038
www.prsa.org

The International Association of Business Communicators offers a variety of resources and opportunities for students who plan on entering the communication profession. For additional information, write to:

International Association of Business Communicators (IABC)
One Hallidie Plaza, Suite 600
San Francisco, CA 94102
www.iabc.com

For information about careers in advertising, contact:

American Association of Advertising Agencies (AAAA)
405 Lexington Avenue, Eighteenth Floor
New York, NY 10174
www.aaaa.org

The American Advertising Federation sponsors an annual student conference, student advertising awards, and a variety of educational opportunities. For more information, contact:

American Advertising Federation (AAF)
1101 Vermont Avenue NW, Suite 500
Washington, DC 20005
www.aaf.org

CHAPTER FOUR

Careers in Law

If there were no bad people, there would be no good lawyers.
—Charles Dickens, *The Old Curiosity Shop*

I
f you're considering a career as a lawyer, you might be imagining a defense attorney like Mark Geragos or a district attorney like Jack McCoy from television's "Law and Order." Or you might have seen Perry Mason, the original television lawyer, in early black-and-white reruns. His clients were always innocent, he always got them off, and he always nabbed the real criminal to boot.

But real life doesn't always follow high-profile cases or the imagination of television writers. If criminal law is the area that interests you, you should know that many of your clients will not be innocent, and you might not be able to get them all off. Some you'd even rather not represent. But, in our justice system, everyone is innocent until proven guilty, and everyone is entitled to legal defense.

Areas of Specialty

Although criminal law is a very popular and much-publicized specialty, it is not the only avenue lawyers can pursue. The more detailed aspects of a lawyer's job depend on his or her position and field of specialization. Even though all lawyers are allowed to represent parties in court, some appear in court more frequently than others. Lawyers who specialize in trial work need an exceptional ability to think quickly and speak with ease and authority, and they must be thoroughly familiar with courtroom rules and strategy. But trial lawyers still spend most of their time outside the courtroom conducting research, interviewing clients and witnesses, and handling other details in preparation for trial.

There are, however, attorneys who may never see the inside of a courtroom. The majority of lawyers are in private practice, where they may concentrate on criminal or civil law. What follows is an overview of each type of law specialization.

Criminal Law

Criminal lawyers represent people who have been charged with crimes. Their responsibility is to argue their clients' cases in courts of law. These attorneys operate their own practices, work for private law firms, or represent clients under the auspices of the public defender's office.

Lawyers who work for state attorneys, general prosecutors, and courts play a key role in the criminal justice system. At the federal level, attorneys investigate cases for the Department of Justice or other agencies. Also, lawyers at every government level help develop programs, draft laws, interpret legislation, establish enforcement procedures, and argue civil and criminal cases on behalf of the government.

Civil Law

In civil law, attorneys assist clients with litigation, wills, trusts, contracts, mortgages, titles, and leases. Some manage personal property as trustees or, as executors, see that provisions of clients' wills are carried out. Others handle only public-interest cases, either civil or criminal, that have a potential impact extending well beyond the individual client or situation. Other lawyers work for legal-aid societies, which are private, nonprofit organizations established to serve disadvantaged people. These lawyers generally handle civil rather than criminal cases. Some other specializations within civil law include:

bankruptcy
corporate law
environmental law
family law
insurance law
intellectual property
international law
probate
real estate law
tax law

Lawyers sometimes are employed full-time by a single client. If the client is a corporation, the lawyer is known as house counsel and usually advises the company about legal questions that arise from its business activities. These questions might involve patents, government regulations, contracts with other companies, property interests, libel issues, or collective-bargaining agreements with unions. Among the entities that employ house counsels are banks and publishing houses.

Government Attorneys

Attorneys employed at the various levels of government comprise another category within the legal profession. The attorney general of any state is the chief law officer of the state. Under the attorney general, hundreds of assistant attorneys general, or district attorneys, as they are often called, work in offices in various cities throughout each state. District attorneys and their staff attorneys are also known as prosecutors. They represent the state in all criminal cases.

Government attorneys represent the state in civil actions, such as the big tobacco lawsuits that surface in the news from time to time. In some states, local prosecutors have an appellate division in each office, and these attorneys handle only appeals. Once in a while, one side or the other in a legal action requests an oral argument, which means that it is time for the appeals attorneys to go to court. If the verdict is overturned, the state often has to retry the case.

Law Clerks

Law clerk can be a misleading title. Many people mistakenly think it refers to someone who is an administrative assistant as opposed to an attorney. But law clerks are, indeed, attorneys. In recent years some have begun using the term *research attorney*, which might be a more fitting description of the position. Sometimes they're called "elbow clerks" because they work at the elbow of the judge, usually for a one- to two-year stint directly out of law school or, for some, as a full-time, professional career. Duties vary depending on the judge you work with, but in general reading briefs, writing notes on them, and conducting research are a law clerk's main responsibilities.

Law clerks must be highly qualified attorneys. Most have graduated in at least the top quarter or higher of their classes. As a full-time career, a job as a law clerk has its pluses and minuses. Salaries are generally much lower than those paid by private law firms, and job security depends on whether the judge you work for stays on the bench. He or she could retire or fail to win reelection, which would mean the end of your job. On the other hand, the hours are fairly normal, and there is usually less stress and competition to deal with than in a busy law firm.

Law Professors

A relatively small number of trained attorneys work in law schools. Most are faculty members who specialize in one or more subjects. Others serve as administrators. Some work full-time in nonacademic settings and teach part-time.

Working Conditions for Lawyers

Lawyers do most of their work in offices, law libraries, and courtrooms. They sometimes meet in clients' homes or places of business and, when necessary, in hospitals or prisons. Many lawyers travel to attend meetings, gather evidence, and appear before courts, legislative bodies, and other authorities.

Salaried lawyers in government and private corporations usually have structured work schedules. Lawyers who are in private practice may work irregular hours while conducting research, conferring with clients, or preparing briefs. Lawyers often work long hours, and of those who regularly work full-time, about half work fifty hours or more per week. They may face particularly heavy pressure when a case is being tried.

Preparation for court includes keeping abreast of the latest laws and judicial decisions. Although legal work generally is not seasonal, the work of tax lawyers and other specialists may be an exception. Because lawyers in private practice often can determine their own workload and the point at which they will retire, many stay in practice well beyond the usual retirement age.

The Role of the Attorney

No matter the setting, whether acting as advocates or prosecutors, all attorneys interpret the law and apply it to specific situations. This requires strong research and communication abilities. Lawyers perform in-depth research into the purposes behind the applicable laws and into the judicial decisions that have been applied to those laws under circumstances similar to those faced by the current client.

Lawyers increasingly use various forms of technology to perform many of their tasks more efficiently. Although all lawyers continue to use law libraries to prepare cases, some supplement conventional printed sources with computer sources, such as the

Internet and legal databases. Software is used to search this legal literature automatically and to identify legal texts relevant to a specific case. In litigation involving many supporting documents, lawyers may use computers to organize and index the material. Lawyers also use electronic filing, videoconferencing, and voice-recognition technology to share information more effectively with other parties involved in a case.

Training and Qualifications

To practice law in the courts of any state or other jurisdiction, an attorney must be licensed, or admitted to its bar, under rules established by the jurisdiction's highest court. All states require that applicants for admission to the bar pass a written bar examination; most states also require applicants to pass a separate written ethics examination. In some cases, lawyers who have been admitted to the bar in one state may be admitted to the bar in another without taking an examination if they meet the latter jurisdiction's standards of good moral character and a specified period of legal experience. In most cases, however, lawyers must pass the bar examination in each state in which they plan to practice. Federal courts set their own qualifications for the attorneys who practice in or before federal courts or agencies.

To qualify for the bar examination in most states, an applicant usually must earn a college degree and graduate from a law school accredited by the American Bar Association (ABA) or the proper state authorities. ABA accreditation signifies that the law school, particularly its library and faculty, meets certain standards developed to promote quality legal education. As of 2005, there were 191 ABA-accredited law schools; others were approved by state authorities only. With certain exceptions, graduates of schools not approved by the ABA are restricted to taking the bar examination and practicing in the state or other jurisdiction in which the school is located; most of these schools are in California. In 2005, seven states—California, Maine, New York, Vermont, Virginia, Washington, and Wyoming—accepted the study of law in a law office as qualification for taking the bar examination; three jurisdictions—California, the District of Columbia, and New Mexico—now accept the study of law by correspondence. Several states require registration and approval of students by the state Board of Law Examiners, either before the students enter law school or during their early years of legal study.

Although there is no nationwide bar examination, forty-eight states, the District of Columbia, Guam, the Northern Mariana Islands, Puerto Rico, and the Virgin Islands require the six-hour Multistate Bar Examination (MBE) as part of the overall bar exam; the MBE is not required in Louisiana or Washington. The MBE covers a broad range of issues, and sometimes a locally prepared state bar examination is given in addition to it. The three-hour Multistate Essay Examination (MEE) is used as part of the bar exam in several states. States vary in their use of MBE and MEE scores.

Many states also require Multistate Performance Testing (MPT) to test the practical skills of beginning lawyers. Requirements vary by state, although the test usually is taken at the same time as the bar exam and is a one-time requirement.

The required college and law school education usually takes seven years of full-time study after high school—four years of undergraduate study followed by three years of law school. Law school applicants must have a bachelor's degree to qualify for admission. To meet the needs of students who can attend only part-time, a number of law schools have night or part-time divisions, which usually require four years of study; about one in ten graduates from ABA-approved schools attended part-time.

Although there is no prelaw major, prospective lawyers should develop proficiency in writing and speaking, reading, researching, analyzing, and thinking logically—all skills needed to succeed both in law school and in the profession. Regardless of major, a multidisciplinary background is recommended. Courses in English, foreign languages, public speaking, government, philosophy, history, economics, mathematics, and computer science are useful, among others. Students interested in a particular aspect of law may find related courses helpful. For example, prospective patent lawyers need a strong background in engineering or science, and future tax lawyers must have extensive knowledge of accounting.

Acceptance by most law schools depends on the applicant's ability to demonstrate an aptitude for the study of law, usually through good undergraduate grades, the Law School Admission Test (LSAT), the quality of the applicant's undergraduate school, any prior work experience, and, sometimes, a personal interview. However, law schools vary in the weight they place on each of these and other factors.

All law schools approved by the ABA require applicants to take the LSAT. Nearly all law schools require applicants to have certified transcripts sent to the Law School Data Assembly Service, which then submits the applicants' LSAT scores and their standardized records of college grades to the law schools of their choice. Both this service and the LSAT are administered by the Law School Admission Council. Competition for admission to many law schools, especially the most prestigious ones, is generally intense, with the number of applicants greatly exceeding the number that can be admitted.

Studies during the first year of law school usually include core courses, such as constitutional law, contracts, property law, torts, civil procedure, and legal writing. In the remaining time, students may elect specialized courses in fields such as tax, labor, or corporate law. Law students often acquire practical experience by participating in school-sponsored legal clinics; in the school's moot court competitions, in which students conduct appellate arguments; in practice trials under the supervision of experienced lawyers and judges; and through research and writing on legal issues for the school's law journal.

A number of law schools have clinical programs in which students gain legal experience through practice trials and projects under the supervision of practicing lawyers and law school faculty. For example, law school clinical programs might include work in legal-aid clinics or on the staff of legislative committees. Part-time or summer clerkships in law firms, government agencies, and corporate legal departments also provide valuable experience. Such training can lead directly to a job after graduation and can help students decide what kind of practice best suits them. Clerkships also may be an important source of financial aid.

In 2004, law school graduates in fifty-two jurisdictions were required to pass the Multistate Professional Responsibility Examination (MPRE), which tests their knowledge of the ABA codes on professional responsibility and judicial conduct. In some states, the MPRE may be taken during law school, usually after completing a course on legal ethics.

Law school graduates receive the degree of juris doctor (J.D.) as the first professional degree. Advanced law degrees may be desirable for those planning to specialize, research, or teach. Some law students pursue joint degree programs, which usually require an additional semester or year of study. Joint degree programs are offered in a number of areas, including law and business administration or public administration.

After graduation, lawyers must keep informed about developments that affect their practices. Currently, forty states and jurisdictions mandate continuing legal education (CLE). Many law schools and state and local bar associations provide continuing education courses that help lawyers stay abreast of recent developments. Some states allow CLE credits to be obtained through participation in seminars on the Internet.

The practice of law involves a great deal of responsibility. Individuals planning careers in law should like to work with people and be able to win the respect and confidence of their clients, associates, and the public. Perseverance, creativity, and reasoning ability also are essential to lawyers, who often analyze complex cases and must grapple with new and unique legal problems.

Advancement and Employment Outlook

Most beginning lawyers start in salaried positions. Newly hired salaried attorneys usually start as associates and work with more experienced lawyers or judges. After several years of gaining responsibilities, some lawyers are admitted to partnership in their firms or go into practice for themselves. Some experienced lawyers are nominated or elected to judgeships. Others become full-time law school faculty or administrators; a growing number of these lawyers have advanced degrees in other fields as well as in law.

Some attorneys use their legal training in administrative or managerial positions in various departments of large corporations. A transfer from a corporation's legal department to another department often is viewed as a way to gain administrative experience and rise in the ranks of management.

Lawyers held about 735,000 jobs in 2004. Approximately three out of four lawyers practiced privately, either as partners in law firms or in solo practices. Most salaried lawyers held positions in government or with corporations or nonprofit organizations. The greatest number of government attorneys were employed at the local level. In the federal government, lawyers work for many different agencies but are concentrated in the Departments of Justice, Treasury, and Defense.

Many salaried lawyers working outside of government are employed as house counsel by public utilities, banks, insurance companies, real estate agencies, manufacturing firms, and other business firms and nonprofit organizations. Some also have part-time, independent practices, while others work part-time as lawyers and full-time in another occupation.

Employment of lawyers is expected to grow between 9 and 17 percent through 2014, primarily as a result of growth in the population and in the general level of business activities. Job growth among lawyers also should result from increasing demand for legal services in such areas as health care, intellectual property, venture capital, energy, environmental, antitrust, and elder law. In addition, the wider availability and affordability of legal clinics should result in increased use of legal services by middle-income people.

However, growth in demand for lawyers may be limited as businesses, in an effort to reduce costs, increasingly use large accounting firms and paralegals to perform some of the same functions that lawyers do. For example, accounting firms may provide benefit counseling for employees, process documents, or handle various other services previously performed by a law firm. Also, mediation and dispute resolution increasingly are being used as alternatives to litigation.

Given the large number of students who graduate from law schools each year, competition for job openings should continue to be strong. Graduates with superior academic records from highly regarded law schools will have the best job opportunities. Perhaps as a result of competition for attorney positions, lawyers are increasingly finding work in nontraditional areas for which legal training is an asset but not normally a requirement, such as administrative, managerial, and business positions in banks, insurance firms, real estate companies, government agencies, and other organizations. Employment opportunities are expected to continue to arise in these organizations at a growing rate.

As in the past, some graduates may have to accept positions in areas outside of their field of interest or for which they feel overqualified. Some recent law school graduates who have been unable to find permanent positions are turning to the growing number of temporary staffing firms that place attorneys in short-term jobs until they are able to secure full-time positions. This service allows companies to hire lawyers on an as-needed basis and permits beginning lawyers to develop practical skills while looking for permanent positions.

Because of the stiff competition for jobs, a law graduate's work experience and geographic mobility assume greater importance. However, while willingness to relocate may be an advantage in getting a job, a lawyer may have to take an additional state bar examination in order to be licensed to practice in a different location. In addition, employers are increasingly seeking graduates who have advanced law degrees and experience in a specialty, such as tax, patent, or admiralty law.

Employment growth for lawyers will continue to be concentrated in salaried jobs, as businesses and all levels of government employ a growing number of staff attorneys and as employment in the legal services industry grows. Most salaried positions are in urban areas where government agencies, law firms, and big corporations are concentrated.

The number of self-employed lawyers is expected to decrease slowly, reflecting the difficulty of establishing a profitable new practice in the face of competition from larger, established law firms. The growing complexity of law, which encourages specialization, along with the cost of maintaining up-to-date legal research materials, also favors larger firms.

For lawyers who wish to work independently, establishing a new practice is probably easiest in small towns and expanding suburban areas. Competition from larger, established law firms is likely to be less keen than in big cities, and new lawyers may find it easier to become known to potential clients.

Some lawyers are adversely affected by cyclical swings in the economy. During recessions, demand declines for some discretionary legal services, such as planning estates, drafting wills, and handling real estate transactions. Also, corporations are less likely to litigate cases when declining sales and profits result in budgetary restrictions. Some corporations and law firms will not hire new attorneys until business improves, and these establishments may even cut staff to contain costs. Several factors, however, mitigate the overall impact of recessions on lawyers; during recessions, for example, individuals and corporations face other legal problems, such as bankruptcies, foreclosures, and divorces requiring legal action.

....

Earnings for Lawyers

Law is a much more demanding profession than most people realize, and it is not always the high-income profession many people think it is. Yes, a lot of attorneys do earn a lot of money. But there are also attorneys running themselves ragged from courtroom to courtroom and barely earning enough to repay their school loans.

Contrary to the experience of John Grisham's hero in *The Firm*, annual salaries of beginning lawyers in private industry average about $60,000. But, in some cases, top graduates from the nation's best law schools can start at more than $100,000 a year.

Factors affecting the salaries offered to new graduates include academic record; type, size, and location of employer; and the specialized educational background desired.

Here's a look at average salaries for new law school graduates working for just nine months in a variety of specializations:

Private practice	$80,000
Business and industry	$60,000
Judicial clerkship and government	$44,700
Higher education	$40,000

Salaries of experienced attorneys vary widely according to the type, size, and location of their employer. Lawyers who own their own practices usually earn less than those who are partners in law firms. Lawyers starting a practice may need to work part-time in other occupations to supplement their income until their practice is well established.

Most salaried lawyers are provided health and life insurance, and contributions are made to retirement plans on their behalf. Lawyers who practice independently are covered only if they arrange and pay for such benefits themselves.

Practicing Law in Canada

In Canada, the legal profession is a self-governing body, regulated in each province by a Law Society. The Law Society determines whether an applicant can be licensed to practice law. The basic procedure for a prospective lawyer is to graduate from an approved law school and complete the bar admission course in the province in which he or she wants to practice.

The academic prerequisite for taking the bar admission course is either graduation from a Canadian university common law program approved by the Law Society or a certificate of qualification issued by the National Committee on Accreditation. There are sixteen universities in Canada that offer law courses approved by the Law Society. A student must meet the requirements of the university in order to study law. An approved law course takes three years to complete and leads to a bachelor of laws (LL.B.) or doctor of jurisprudence (J.D.) degree.

The specific requirements for the bar admission course differ among the provinces, but in general, the course is comprised of three phases: a skills phase, a substantive/procedural phase, and an articling phase. The skills and substantive/procedural phases usually run from eight to ten weeks each. The articling phase (the development of practical legal skills under the supervision of a lawyer) can last ten to twelve months. The bar examination is taken upon successful completion of the bar admission course. All lawyers must join the Law Society in the province where they practice.

Paralegals

While lawyers assume ultimate responsibility for legal work, they often delegate many of their tasks to paralegals. In fact, paralegals, also called legal assistants, are assuming a growing range of tasks in legal offices and perform many of the same tasks as lawyers. However, they are still explicitly prohibited from carrying out duties that are considered to be the practice of law, such as setting legal fees, giving legal advice, and presenting cases in court.

One of a paralegal's most important tasks is helping lawyers prepare for closings, hearings, trials, and corporate meetings. Paralegals investigate the facts of cases and ensure that all relevant information is considered. They also identify appropriate laws, judicial decisions, legal articles, and other materials that are relevant to assigned cases. After they analyze and organize the information, paralegals may prepare written reports that attorneys use in determining how cases should be handled. When attorneys decide to file lawsuits on behalf of clients, paralegals may help prepare the legal arguments, draft pleadings and motions to be filed with the court, obtain affidavits, and assist attorneys during trials. Paralegals also organize and track files of all important case documents and make them available and easily accessible to attorneys.

Paralegals perform a number of other vital functions in addition to this preparatory work. For example, they help draft contracts, mortgages, separation agreements, and instruments of trust. They also may assist in preparing tax returns and planning estates. Some paralegals coordinate the activities of other law office employees and maintain financial records. Additional tasks vary, depending on the employer.

Most paralegals are employed by law firms, corporate legal departments, and various government offices. They can work in many different areas of the law, including litigation, personal injury, corporate law, criminal law, employee benefits, intellectual property, labor law, bankruptcy, immigration, family law, and real estate. As the law has become more complex, paralegals have responded by becoming more specialized. Within specialties, functions often are broken down further so that paralegals may focus on a specific area. For example, paralegals specializing in labor law may concentrate exclusively on employee benefits.

The duties of paralegals also differ widely with the type of organization in which they are employed. Paralegals who work for corporations often assist attorneys with employee contracts, shareholder agreements, stock-option plans, and employee benefit plans. They also may help prepare and file annual financial reports, maintain corporate minutes, and prepare forms to secure loans for the corporation. Paralegals often monitor and review government regulations to ensure that the corporation is aware of new requirements and is operating within the law. Increasingly, experienced paralegals are assuming additional supervisory responsibilities, such as overseeing team projects and serving as a communications link between the team and the corporation.

The duties of paralegals who work in the public sector usually vary within each agency. In general, paralegals analyze legal material for internal use, maintain reference files, conduct research for attorneys, and collect and analyze evidence for agency hearings. They may prepare informative or explanatory material on laws, agency regulations, and agency policy for general use by the agency and the public. Paralegals employed in community legal-service projects help the poor, the aged, and others who are in need of legal assistance. They file forms, conduct research, prepare documents, and, when authorized by law, may represent clients at administrative hearings.

Paralegals in small and medium-size law firms usually perform a variety of duties that require a general knowledge of the law. For example, a paralegal may research judicial decisions on improper police arrests one day, then help prepare a mortgage contract the next. Those employed by large law firms, government agencies, and corporations, however, are more likely to specialize in one aspect of the law.

As is the case with attorneys, familiarity with computers and technical knowledge has become essential to paralegal work. Computer software packages and the Internet are used to search legal literature stored in computer databases and on CD-ROM. In litigation involving many supporting documents, paralegals usually use computer databases to retrieve, organize, and index various materials. Imaging software allows paralegals to scan documents directly into a database, while billing programs help them to track hours for billing to clients. Computer software packages also are used to perform tax computations and explore the consequences of various tax strategies for clients.

Training and Qualifications

There are several ways to become a paralegal. The most common is through a community college paralegal program that leads to an associate's degree. The other common method of entry, mainly for those who already have a college degree, is through a program that leads to a certification in paralegal studies. A small number of schools also offer bachelor's and master's degrees in paralegal studies. Some employers train paralegals on the job, hiring college graduates with no legal experience or promoting experienced legal secretaries. Other entrants have experience in a technical field that is useful to law firms, such as a background in tax preparation for tax and estate practice or experience in criminal justice, nursing, or health administration for personal injury practice.

Approximately one thousand colleges and universities, law schools, and proprietary schools offer formal paralegal training programs. About one-quarter of these are approved by the American Bar Association (ABA). Although many programs do not require such approval, graduation from an ABA-approved program can enhance your employment opportunities. The requirements for admission to these programs vary. Some require specific college courses or a bachelor's degree. Others accept high school graduates or those with legal experience, and a few schools require completion of standardized tests and personal interviews.

Paralegal programs include two-year associate's degree programs, four-year bachelor's degree programs, and certificate programs that can take only a few months to complete. Most certificate programs provide intensive and, in some cases, specialized paralegal training for individuals who already hold college degrees, while associate's and bachelor's degree programs usually combine paralegal training with courses in other academic subjects. The quality of paralegal training programs varies; the better programs usually include job placement services. Prospective students should examine the experiences of recent graduates before enrolling in a paralegal program.

Programs generally offer courses introducing students to the legal applications of computers, including how to perform legal research on the Internet. Many offer internships through which students gain practical experience by working for several months in a private law firm, the office of a public defender or attorney general, a bank, a corporate legal department, a legal-aid organization, or a government agency. Experience gained in internships is an asset when seeking a job after graduation.

Although most employers do not require certification, earning a voluntary certificate from a professional society may offer advantages in the labor market. The National Association of Legal Assistants (NALA), for example, has established standards for certification requiring various combinations of education and experience. Paralegals who meet these standards are eligible to take a two-day examination, given three times each year at several regional testing centers. Those who pass this examination may use the Certified Legal Assistant (CLA) designation. NALA also offers an advanced paralegal certification for those who want to specialize in other areas of the law. In addition, the Paralegal Advanced Competency Exam, administered through the National Federation of Paralegal Associations, offers professional recognition to paralegals with a bachelor's degree and at least two years of experience. Those who pass this examination may use the Registered Paralegal (RP) designation.

Paralegals must be able to document and present their findings and opinions to their supervising attorney. They need to understand legal terminology and have good research and investigative skills. Familiarity with the operation and applications of computers in legal research and litigation support also is important. Paralegals should stay informed of new developments in the laws that affect their areas of practice. Participation in continuing legal education seminars allows paralegals to maintain and expand their knowledge of the law.

Because paralegals frequently deal with the public, they should be courteous and uphold the ethical standards of the legal profession. The National Association of Legal Assistants, the National Federation of Paralegal Associations, and a few states have established ethical guidelines for paralegals to follow.

Paralegals usually are given more responsibilities and require less supervision as they gain work experience. Experienced paralegals who work in large law firms, corporate legal departments, or government agencies may supervise and delegate assignments to other paralegals and clerical staff. Advancement opportunities also include promotion to managerial and other law-related positions within the firm or corporate legal department. However, some paralegals find it easier to move to another law firm when seeking increased responsibility or advancement.

Earnings

Earnings for paralegals and legal assistants vary greatly, depending on education, training, experience, the type and size of employer, and the geographic location of the job. In general, paralegals who work for large law firms or in large metropolitan areas earn more than those who work for smaller firms or in less populated regions. Many paralegals receive bonuses in addition to their salaries. In May 2004, full-time wage and salary paralegals and legal assistants had median annual earnings, including bonuses, of $39,130. The middle 50 percent earned between $31,040 and $49,950. The top 10 percent earned more than $61,390, while the bottom 10 percent earned less than $25,360. Median annual earnings in the industries employing the largest numbers of paralegals in May 2004 were as follows:

Federal government	$59,370
Local government	$38,260
Legal services	$37,870
State government	$34,910

Meet a Professional

If you think your competitive spirit would be at home practicing law, read the following account to see whether you are right.

Nicole D. Blake, Self-Employed Attorney

Nicole D. Blake is a self-employed lawyer in Seattle, Washington. She received her B.A. in political science from Loyola University in Chicago, then earned her J.D. from DePaul University in Chicago.

Nicole has been a lawyer since 1991. "I always wanted to help others," she says. "I don't have a mathematical mind, but I do have a great ability and proclivity for argument, so it seemed an obvious career path. Also, I come from a family that stressed education. Several family members had already followed a career path in law. In fact, one of my cousins was the first blind lawyer admitted to practice in Chicago."

Nicole's first job after law school was working as a public defender. In this position, she worked in dependency law, which involved defending parents against losing their rights when the state has removed their children to foster care. The caseload was high, which made the job difficult. Following her work as a public defender, Nicole did some nonlegal work as an adoption social worker for a nonprofit agency. She worked at that job for about eighteen months before being laid off.

In her private practice, Nicole focuses mainly on dependency law and its related areas of divorce, adoption, and other aspects of family law. Her daily schedule is varied, since something unexpected happens on most days. However, Nicole says that certain aspects of her day are constant. For instance, she spends a good deal of time returning telephone calls. "I rarely answer the phone because this is one of the few ways that I can remain in charge of my own time," Nicole explains. "Another common responsibility is to attend hearings, often in more than one courthouse in more than one city at a time. Usually I work on at least one legal writing per day. Filing paperwork or figuring out what to do with any certain piece of paper is the time waster that I resent the most."

Nicole enjoys working with clients, especially when a case is going well. Things become difficult, however, when clients don't understand her role or the limitations of the law to resolve their issues.

"As a solo practitioner, I enjoy being my own boss, organizing my own schedule," Nicole says. "Then again, I dislike organizing my own schedule and keeping my own books."

Nicole advises anyone who is interested in practicing law to participate in debate teams in high school and college. Her final word of advice: "Study instead of going to parties so that you can get into one of the best possible law schools."

For More Information

The American Bar Association provides information about the law schools approved by the ABA, bar admissions requirements, and other information on legal education.

American Bar Association (ABA)
321 North Clark Street
Chicago, IL 60610
www.abanet.org

For educational and career opportunities for attorneys in Canada, contact:

Canadian Bar Association
500–865 Carling Avenue
Ottawa, ON K1S 5S8
Canada
www.cba.org

Federation of Law Societies of Canada
445 Boulevard Saint-Laurent, Suite 480
Montreal, QC H2Y 2Y7
Canada
www.flsc.ca

Information on the LSAT, the Law School Data Assembly Service, applying to law school, financial aid for law students, and law schools in the U.S. and Canada may be obtained from:

Law School Admission Council
www.lsac.org

General information on a career as a paralegal and a list of paralegal training programs approved by the American Bar Association may be purchased from:

Division for Legal Services
American Bar Association
321 North Clark Street
Chicago, IL 60610
www.abanet.org/legalservices/paralegals

For information on paralegal certification, training programs in specific states, and standards and guidelines, contact:

National Association of Legal Assistants, Inc.
1516 South Boston, Suite 200
Tulsa, OK 74119
www.nala.org

National Federation of Paralegal Associations
PO Box 2016
Edmonds, WA 98020
www.paralegals.org

In Canada, visit the following website:

Canadian Association of Paralegals
www.caplegal.ca

CHAPTER FIVE

Careers in Research

> *Any sufficiently advanced technology*
> *is indistinguishable from magic.*
> —Arthur C. Clarke, *The Lost Worlds of 2001*

re you fascinated by news reports about avian flu and mad cow disease? Is it your secret dream to find a cure for cystic fibrosis or to put an end to the ravages of cancer? Do you want a better understanding of our relationships to other living creatures? If you are passionate about discovering cures or insuring the safety of the food we eat and the medicines we take, then your competitive spirit might be well served in a research career.

Research Careers in the Biological and Medical Sciences

Many biological scientists and virtually all medical scientists work in the area of research and development. Some conduct basic research to increase our knowledge of living organisms. Others, in applied research, use knowledge gained through basic research to develop new medicines, increase crop yields, and improve the environment.

Biological and medical scientists who conduct research usually work in laboratories using electron microscopes, computers, thermal cyclers, and a wide variety of other equipment. Some research professionals may conduct experiments on laboratory animals or greenhouse plants. A number of biological scientists perform a substantial amount of research outside of laboratories. For example, a botanist may do research in tropical rain forests to see what plants grow there, or an ecologist may study how a forest area recovers after a fire.

Some biological and medical scientists work in management or administration. They may plan and administer programs for testing foods and drugs, for example, or direct activities at zoos or botanical gardens. Some biological scientists work as consultants to business firms or to government, while others test and inspect foods, drugs, and other products or write for technical publications. Some work in sales and service jobs for companies that manufacture chemicals or other technical products.

Advances in basic biological knowledge, especially at the genetic and molecular levels, continue to spur the field of biotechnology forward. Using this technology, biological and medical scientists manipulate the genetic material of animals or plants, attempting to make organisms more productive or disease resistant.

The first application of this technology occurred in the medical and pharmaceutical areas. Many substances that were not previously available in large quantities are now being produced by biotechnological means—some may be useful in treating cancer and other diseases. Advances in biotechnology have opened up research opportunities in almost all areas of biology, including commercial applications in agriculture and the food and chemical industries.

Career Opportunities

Most biological scientists are classified by the types of organisms they study or by the specific activities they perform, although recent advances in the understanding of basic life processes at the molecular and cellular levels have blurred some traditional classifications.

Aquatic Biologists. Aquatic biologists study plants and animals that live in water. Marine biologists study saltwater organisms, and limnologists study freshwater organisms. Marine biologists are sometimes called oceanographers, but oceanography refers to the study of the physical characteristics of oceans and the ocean floor.

Biochemists. Biochemists study the chemical composition of living things. They try to understand the complex chemical combinations and reactions involved in metabolism, reproduction, growth, and heredity. Much of the work in biotechnology is done by biochemists and molecular biologists because this technology involves understanding the complex chemistry of life.

Botanists. Botanists study plants and their environments. Some study all aspects of plant life; others specialize in areas such as the identification and classification of plants, the structures and functions of plant parts, the biochemistry of plant processes, the causes and cures of plant diseases, and the geological ancestries of plants.

Ecologists. Ecologists study the relationships among organisms and between organisms and their environments. They also study the effects of influences such as population size, pollutants, rainfall, temperature, and altitude.

Medical Scientists. Biological scientists who conduct biomedical research are usually called medical scientists. Medical scientists working on basic research delve into the functioning of normal biological systems in order to understand the causes of and to discover treatments for diseases and other health problems. They often try to identify the kinds of changes in cells, chromosomes, or genes that signal the development of medical problems, such as different types of cancer.

After identifying clues to health problems, medical scientists may then work on the treatment of problems. For example, a medical scientist involved in cancer research might try to formulate a combination of drugs that lessen the effects of the disease. Medical scientists who have a medical degree might then administer the drugs to patients in clinical trials, monitor their reactions, and observe the results. (Those who do not have a medical degree normally collaborate with a medical doctor who deals directly with patients.) The medical scientist might then return to the laboratory to examine the results and, if necessary, to adjust the dosage levels to reduce negative side effects or try to induce even better results. In addition to using basic research to develop treatments for health problems, medical scientists attempt to discover ways to prevent health problems from developing, such as affirming the link between smoking and increased risk of lung cancer, or alcoholism and liver disease.

Microbiologists. Microbiologists investigate the growth and characteristics of microscopic organisms such as bacteria, algae, or fungi. Medical microbiologists study the relationships between organisms and disease or the effects of antibiotics on microorganisms. Other microbiologists may specialize in environmental, food, agricultural, or industrial microbiology; virology (the study of viruses); or immunology (the study of mechanisms that fight infections). Many microbiologists use biotechnology as they advance knowledge of cell reproduction and human disease.

Physiologists. Physiologists study life functions of plants and animals, both in the whole organism and at the cellular or molecular level, under normal and abnormal conditions. They may specialize in functions such as growth, reproduction, photosynthesis, respiration, or movement, or they may focus on the physiology of a certain area or system of the organism.

Zoologists. Zoologists study animals—their origins, behaviors, diseases, and life processes. Some experiment with or observe the behaviors of live animals in controlled or natural surroundings, while others dissect dead animals to study their structures. Zoologists are usually identified by the animal group they study, such as ornithologists (birds), mammalogists (mammals), herpetologists (reptiles), and ichthyologists (fish).

Training and Qualifications

For biological scientists, the doctoral degree generally is required for college teaching, independent research, and for advancement to administrative positions. A master's degree is sufficient for some jobs in applied research and for jobs in management, inspection, sales, and service. Some graduates with a bachelor's degree start as biological scientists in testing and inspection or get jobs related to biological science, such as technical sales or service representatives. In some cases, graduates with bachelor's degrees are able to work in a laboratory environment on their own projects, but this is unusual. Some may work as research assistants. Others become biological technicians or medical laboratory technologists. Many with bachelor's degrees in biology enter medical, dental, veterinary, or other health profession schools.

In addition to required courses in chemistry and biology, undergraduate biological science majors usually study allied disciplines such as mathematics, physics, engineering, and computer science. Computer courses are essential because employers prefer job applicants who are able to apply computer skills to modeling and simulation tasks and to operate computerized laboratory equipment, particularly in emerging fields such as bioinformatics.

Most colleges and universities offer bachelor's degrees in biological science, and many offer advanced degrees. Curricula for advanced degrees often emphasize a subfield such as microbiology or botany, but not all universities offer all curricula. Larger universities frequently have separate departments specializing in different areas of biological science. For example, a program in botany might cover agronomy, horticulture, or plant pathology. Advanced degree programs include classroom and fieldwork, laboratory research, and a thesis or dissertation.

Biological scientists should be able to work independently or as part of a team and be able to communicate clearly and concisely, both orally and in writing. Those in private industry, especially those who aspire to management or administrative positions, should possess strong business and communication skills and be familiar with regulatory issues and marketing and management techniques. Those doing field research in remote areas must have physical stamina. Biological scientists also must have patience and self-discipline to conduct long and detailed research projects.

Biological scientists with a Ph.D. often take temporary postdoctoral research positions that provide specialized research experience. Postdoctoral positions may offer the opportunity to publish research findings. A solid record of published research is essential in obtaining a permanent position involving basic research, especially for those seeking a permanent college or university faculty position. In private industry, some may become managers or administrators within the field of biology; others leave biology for nontechnical managerial, administrative, or sales jobs.

A Ph.D. degree in a biological science is the minimum education required for most prospective medical scientists, except epidemiologists, because the work of medical scientists is almost entirely research oriented. A Ph.D. qualifies one to conduct research on basic life processes or on particular medical problems or diseases and to analyze and interpret the results of experiments on patients.

Some medical scientists obtain a medical degree instead of a Ph.D. but may not be licensed physicians because they have not taken the state licensing examination or completed a residency program, typically because they prefer research to clinical practice. Medical scientists who administer drug or gene therapy to human patients, or who otherwise interact medically with patients (such as drawing blood, excising tissue, or performing other invasive procedures) must be licensed physicians. To be licensed, physicians must graduate from an accredited medical school, pass a licensing examination, and complete one to seven years of graduate medical education. It is particularly helpful for medical scientists to earn both Ph.D. and medical degrees.

Students planning careers as medical scientists should have a bachelor's degree in a biological science. In addition to required courses in chemistry and biology, undergraduates should study allied disciplines, such as mathematics, engineering, physics, and computer science, or courses in their field of interest. Once they have completed undergraduate studies, they can then select a specialty area for their advanced degree, such as cytology, bioinformatics, genomics, or pathology. In addition to formal education, medical scientists usually spend several years in a postdoctoral position before they apply for permanent jobs. Postdoctoral work provides valuable laboratory experience, including experience in specific processes and techniques such as gene splicing, which is transferable to other research projects. In some institutions, the postdoctoral position can lead to a permanent job.

Medical scientists should be able to work independently or as part of a team and be able to communicate clearly and concisely, both orally and in writing. Those in private industry, especially those who aspire to consulting and administrative positions, should possess strong communication skills so that they can provide instruction and advice to physicians and other health care professionals.

The minimum educational requirement for epidemiology is a master's degree from a school of public health. Some jobs require a Ph.D. or medical degree, depending on the work performed. Epidemiologists who work in hospitals and health care centers usually must have earned a medical degree with specific training in infectious diseases. Currently, approximately 140 infectious disease training programs exist in forty-two states.

Some employees in research epidemiology positions are required to be licensed physicians because they must administer drugs to patients in clinical trials. Epidemiologists who perform laboratory tests often require the knowledge and expertise of a licensed physician in order to administer drugs to patients in clinical trials.

The Association for Professionals in Infection Control and Epidemiology offers continuing education courses and certification programs in infection prevention and control and applied epidemiology. To become certified as an infection control professional, applicants are required by a certification board to pass an examination for a one-time fee. Certification is recommended for those seeking advancement and for those seeking to upgrade their knowledge in a rapidly evolving field.

Earnings for Biological and Medical Scientists

According to the National Association of Colleges and Employers, beginning salary offers in July 2005 for bachelor's degree recipients in biological and life sciences averaged $31,258 a year.

In 2004, median annual earnings for microbiologists were $54,840. Median annual earnings for zoologists and wildlife biologists were $50,330. Biochemists and biophysicists earned a median annual salary of $68,950; those employed in scientific research and development services earned $73,900.

In the federal government in 2005, general biological scientists in nonsupervisory, supervisory, and managerial positions earned an average salary of $69,908; microbiologists, $80,798; ecologists, $72,021; physiologists, $93,208; geneticists, $85,170; zoologists, $101,601; and botanists, $62,207.

Median annual earnings of medical scientists, except epidemiologists, were $61,320 in May 2004. The middle 50 percent of these workers earned between $44,120 and $86,830. The lowest 10 percent earned less than $33,030, and the highest 10 percent earned more than $114,360. Median annual earnings in the industries employing the largest numbers of medical scientists in May 2004 were as follows:

Pharmaceutical and medicine manufacturing	$76,800
Scientific research and development services	$65,110
General medical and surgical hospitals	$55,410
Colleges, universities, and professional schools	$45,600

Median annual earnings of epidemiologists were $54,800 in May 2004. The middle 50 percent earned between $45,320 and $67,160. The lowest 10 percent earned less than $36,130, and the highest 10 percent earned more than $82,310.

Meet Some Biological and Medical Science Research Professionals

Read the following accounts of a toxicologist and a medical technologist to see if you have what it takes to work in this interesting field.

Amadeo J. Pesce, Ph.D.

Dr. Amadeo Pesce serves as the director of the toxicology laboratory and professor of experimental medicine at the University of Cincinnati Hospital. He has been associated with the University of Cincinnati for the past thirty years.

Dr. Pesce earned a B.S. in biology at the Massachusetts Institute of Technology, followed by a Ph.D. in biochemistry from Brandeis University. He served his postdoctoral fellowship at the University of Illinois at Urbana-Champaign and is board certified by the American Board for Clinical Chemistry, which requires five years of experience and successful completion of an examination. Dr. Pesce says that he always knew he was interested in medical research, so his studies were always focused on achieving that career goal.

Most of Dr. Pesce's work is conducted as part of a team of researchers. The composition of the team may change depending on the project and may include postdoctoral fellows, part- or full-time technologists, pathologists, mathematicians, psychiatrists, substance-abuse counselors, and other medical and scientific professionals.

Dr. Pesce and his team usually work on several projects simultaneously. He describes a time when the team was involved in helping with clinical trials in developing methods of measurement for different projects. The goal of one study was to help pace patients by monitoring the effectiveness of the drug AZT, which is used in the treatment of AIDS. The research team developed the technology to measure the concentration of drugs inside the cell and worked very closely with the clinician in the clinical trials that were being conducted.

Another project involved the study of developing agents to help combat substance abuse by reducing the cravings that make people want to continue to use drugs. In this situation, the team worked with a group of psychiatrists and substance-abuse counselors who provided specimens from the patients for the researchers to monitor.

"In addition to the hours spent in the laboratory, a considerable portion of my time is spent thinking and writing," Dr. Pesce says. "One must think things through and be able to communicate them effectively and efficiently in order for the research to have meaning. And, as I convey to my students, if it's not written down, it was never done."

In his capacity as administrator, Dr. Pesce has other responsibilities in addition to his research. He supervises a postdoctoral fellow and handles personnel and administrative issues. He now keeps fairly regular working hours, but for many years Dr. Pesce worked from 7 A.M. until 10 P.M., five days a week. But that doesn't mean that he took weekends off—the other two days of the week, he worked eight to ten hours.

Dr. Pesce explains the reasons for this intense schedule. "This was not required, but just my own enthusiasm showing, based upon my decision to be one of the four most recognized authorities in the field. So I set on a path of learning all I could and then proceeded to put out a series of books (eighteen) about the field. This required an immense amount of work. I tell everyone that I did this to become rich and famous. (My children always told me to skip the fame!) But as it turns out, all I got was the fame. However, even though I didn't make the money I had hoped for, it has still been very rewarding. Fans as far away as Australia have asked me to sign their copies of my books."

In addition to fame, Dr. Pesce cites other rewards of his challenging career. The first is the accomplishment of developing a theory and finding supporting data. This is particularly satisfying because research projects are funded by grants for which investigators must show results by a certain date in order to receive funding for additional projects.

The downside of the job, according to Dr. Pesce, is when a paper is rejected by peer reviewers, especially when he knows that his results are correct and the review is not. Despite this, however, he is proud to have done some pioneering work that has yielded rewarding results that help others.

As an example of this, Dr. Pesce recounts a project in which his team developed a way of examining cancer in mice. He received a letter commending him on the work from a colleague working in cancer research, and he feels greatly rewarded to know that someone thinks highly enough of his team's work to build on their results.

Another of the team's accomplishments involved devising a way to cut the cost of drugs used to treat transplant patients from $6,000 a year to $1,200. With this reduction in cost, developing countries could afford the drugs, which was not possible before.

Dr. Pesce advises that a Ph.D. is essential to a successful research career. He also credits having an understanding partner as adding to his success. In addition, he says, "Since it is so important to be able to interact with people, exchange ideas, and get them to help with particular areas of your project, you must have the ability to get along with all kinds of people. You have to be aware of what issues others have and be able to accommodate them so they'll accommodate you in return. I have found that this is the proper approach to a successful collaboration. It's not unlike working with others on a book or any other project in which a number of people need to extend themselves in order to fulfill a common goal."

Dennis J. Ernst, M.T.

Dennis J. Ernst is director of the Center for Phlebotomy Education. He is a medical technologist, certified by the American Society of Clinical Pathologists since 1978. He describes his start in the field and his job as a clinical microbiologist at the University of Louisville Hospital in Louisville, Kentucky. "How I got started may be broken down into two parts—what attracted me to a career in the health sciences and what attracted me to a career as a medical technologist," Dennis says. "The answers are completely different and say as much about the educational process as they do about my impatience with it."

Dennis's mother was a registered nurse, and his earliest memories were inspired by her dedication to caring for the sick and the satisfaction she received from her work. "I came to know that caring for the sick was a noble and rewarding thing. I saw her as someone who had been blessed by fate to see and know the inner workings of the human body, and for me to be so blessed when I came of age was an intriguing prospect."

Dennis studied science in high school and enrolled in the premed program at Albion College in Albion, Michigan. Unfortunately, Dennis's scores on the science placement exam that he took during his first week of classes indicated that he was not likely to succeed in the premed program. In addition, his advisor informed him that he was poorly prepared to major in any science curriculum.

Dennis was stunned by this news and felt that if he could not major in science, he didn't want to be in school at all. He describes himself as "too ignorant to take his advice and too stubborn to pursue another major." With this attitude, Dennis decided to prove both the advisor and the placement tests wrong. He majored in biology but only had mediocre grades, far below what he needed to enter medical school. Although he was still interested in science, his grade point average eliminated medical school and most other high-profile careers.

"By now the struggle had been long and hard, and I was wearing thin on persistence," Dennis recalls. "I had experienced enough of education but still needed to emerge with a face-saving career of some security. The allied health fields presented many offerings but most required more postgraduate study than I had the will to endure. Then my advisor recommended medical technology, the study of blood and disease. It was perfect! I could get that inside peek at the inner workings of the human body that I still craved and with only one year of postgraduate study. I applied for internships and was accepted."

Medical technology involves the laboratory testing of body fluids and tissues for disease. The field includes many subcategories, all of which Dennis has worked at in varying degrees. As a clinical microbiologist in a university hospital, he tests blood, tissues, and body fluids for microorganisms that cause infection. He identifies the microorganisms and recommends antibiotics to fight them. His work also includes immunology, which is research for the presence of disease-fighting antibodies.

Dennis works four eight-hour days a week. A typical day begins with retrieving and collating data that is printed by an automated instrument that works throughout the night to identify microorganisms by species. The data is obtained from patient cultures isolated the previous day. After identification, technologists determine the best antibiotic therapy to be used against the particular organism.

Dennis enters the collated information into the hospital computer system and phones any results that indicated life-threatening conditions to the appropriate physician for immediate treatment. He then sets up newly isolated organisms for the same automated, overnight testing. Dennis is also responsible for the maintenance of his automated equipment and for quality control processes that assure his analytical systems are functioning properly.

Working as a clinical microbiologist carries the risk of infection, but this is minimized with proper and consistent use of personal protective devices such as gowns, gloves, and face shields. Dennis says that the work can be hectic when the hospital is full, but there are times when the patient population is low and the work is light. Overtime is not permitted, so any time spent working more than his scheduled hours must be offset by working proportionally less on another day.

Nearly all of Dennis's coworkers at the hospital have either associate's or bachelor's degrees, and all are certified laboratory professionals in some capacity. The laboratory assistants who prepare the specimens for bacterial isolation and perform many nontechnical tasks are high school graduates who have received on-the-job training.

Dennis describes the most satisfying aspect of his work as the collaboration that exists among his colleagues. He describes both the level of cooperation and the department's goal-oriented momentum as high.

"Anyone interested in a career in the allied health sciences should consider medical technology for the insights it offers into the inner workings of the human body," Dennis says. "Here one finds the constant discovery of the body's beauty and complexity that I hungered for as the young, observant son of a nurse. The intrigue has never ceased. Applications of the skills learned in training are many and varied, rendering the possibility of job burnout in this career remote. However, because of the sweeping application of managed care strategies in health care today, medical technology as a career has changed from one of promised permanence to one that is, at best, a stepping-stone to a more secure and respected calling."

Research Careers in the Physical Sciences

The physical sciences also provide many options for competitive spirits who are interested in research. Here are descriptions of some of the areas that offer employment possibilities.

Chemists

Chemists search for and use new knowledge about chemicals, which comprise everything in the environment, whether naturally occurring or of human design. Chemical research has led to the discovery and development of new and improved synthetic fibers, paints, adhesives, drugs, cosmetics, electronic components, lubricants, and thousands of other products. Chemists also develop processes such as improved oil refining and petrochemical processing that save energy and reduce pollution. Research on the chemistry of living things spurs advances in medicine, agriculture, food processing, and other fields.

Many chemists work in research and development (R&D). In basic research, they investigate properties, composition, and structure of matter and the laws that govern the combination of elements and reactions of substances. In applied R&D, they create new products and processes or improve existing ones, often using knowledge gained from basic research. For example, synthetic rubber and plastics resulted from research on small molecules uniting to form large ones, a process called polymerization. R&D

chemists and materials scientists use computers and a wide variety of sophisticated laboratory instrumentation for modeling and simulation in their work.

Using computers to analyze complex data, chemists can practice combinatorial chemistry, the technique that makes and tests large quantities of chemical compounds simultaneously to find those with certain desired properties. Combinatorial chemistry has allowed chemists to produce thousands of compounds more quickly and inexpensively than was formerly possible and assisted in the completion of the sequencing of human genes. Today, specialty chemists, such as medicinal and organic chemists, are working with life scientists to translate this knowledge into new drugs.

Chemists also work in production and quality control in chemical manufacturing plants. They prepare instructions for plant workers that specify ingredients, mixing times, and temperatures for each stage in the process. They also monitor automated processes to ensure proper product yield and test samples of raw materials or finished products to ensure that they meet industry and government standards, including regulations governing pollution. Chemists report and document test results and analyze those results in hopes of improving existing theories or developing new test methods.

Many chemists specialize. Analytical chemists determine the structure, composition, and nature of substances by examining and identifying their various elements or compounds. These chemists are absolutely crucial to the pharmaceutical industry because pharmaceutical companies need to know the identity of compounds that they hope to turn into drugs. Furthermore, analytical chemists study the relations and interactions of the parts of compounds and develop analytical techniques. They also identify the presence and concentration of chemical pollutants in air, water, and soil.

Organic chemists study the chemistry of the vast number of carbon compounds that make up all living things. Organic chemists synthesize elements or simple compounds to create new compounds or substances that have different properties and applications; they have developed many commercial products, such as drugs, plastics, and elastomers (elastic substances similar to rubber). Inorganic chemists study compounds consisting primarily of elements other than carbon, such as those in electronic components.

Physical and theoretical chemists study the physical characteristics of atoms and molecules and the theoretical properties of matter and investigate how chemical reactions work. Their research may result in new and better energy sources. Macromolecular chemists study the behavior of atoms and molecules. Medicinal chemists study the structural properties of compounds intended for applications to human medicine.

Materials chemists study and develop new materials to improve existing products or make new ones. In fact, virtually all chemists are involved in this quest in one way or another. Developments in the field of chemistry that involve life sciences will expand, resulting in more interaction among biologists, engineers, computer specialists, and chemists.

Physicists and Astronomers

Physicists explore and identify basic principles governing the structure and behavior of matter, the generation and transfer of energy, and the interaction of matter and energy. Some physicists use these principles in theoretical areas, such as the nature of time and the origin of the universe; others apply their physics knowledge to practical areas, such as the development of advanced materials, electronic and optical devices, and medical equipment.

Physicists design and perform experiments with lasers, cyclotrons, telescopes, mass spectrometers, and other equipment. Based on observations and analysis, they attempt to discover the laws that describe the forces of nature, such as gravity, electromagnetism, and nuclear interactions. They also find ways to apply physical laws and theories to problems in nuclear energy, electronics, optics, materials, communications, aerospace technology, navigation equipment, and medical instrumentation. Most physicists work in research and development. Some do basic research to increase scientific knowledge. Physicists who conduct applied research build upon the discoveries made through basic research and work to develop new devices, products, and processes. For instance, basic research in solid-state physics led to the development of transistors and then to the integrated circuits used in computers.

Physicists also design research equipment. This equipment often has additional unanticipated uses. For example, lasers are used in surgery; microwave devices are used for ovens; and measuring instruments can analyze blood or the chemical content of foods. A small number of physicists work in inspection, testing, quality control, and other production-related jobs in industry.

Much physics research is done in small or medium-size laboratories. However, experiments in plasma, nuclear, and high energy and some other areas of physics require extremely large, expensive equipment such as particle accelerators. Physicists in these subfields often work in large teams. Although physics research may require extensive experimentation in laboratories, research physicists still spend time in offices planning, recording, analyzing, and reporting on research.

Physicists generally specialize in one of many subfields—elementary particle physics, nuclear physics, atomic and molecular physics, physics of condensed matter (solid-state physics), optics, acoustics, plasma physics, or the physics of fluids. Some specialize in a subdivision of one of these subfields; for example, within condensed-matter physics, specialties include superconductivity, crystallography, and semiconductors. However, all physics subfields involve the same fundamental principles, so specialties may overlap, and physicists may switch from one subfield to another. Also, growing numbers of physicists work in combined fields, such as biophysics, chemical physics, and geophysics. Astronomy is sometimes considered a subfield of physics. Astronomers use the principles of physics and mathematics to learn about the fundamental nature of the universe, including the sun, moon, planets, stars, and galaxies. They also apply their knowledge to problems in navigation and space flight.

Almost all astronomers conduct research. Some are theoreticians, working on the laws that govern the structure and evolution of astronomical objects. Others analyze large quantities of data gathered by observatories and satellites and write scientific papers or reports on their findings. Some astronomers actually operate large space- or ground-based telescopes, usually as part of a team. However, astronomers may spend only a few weeks each year making observations with optical telescopes, radio telescopes, and other instruments.

For many years, satellites and other space-based instruments, such as the Hubble space telescope, have provided prodigious amounts of astronomical data. New technology resulting in improvements in analytical techniques and instruments, such as computers and optical telescopes and mounts, is leading to a resurgence in ground-based research. A small number of astronomers work in museums housing planetariums. These astronomers develop and revise programs presented to the public and may direct planetarium operations.

Geologists and Geophysicists

Geologists and geophysicists, known as geoscientists, study the composition, structure, and other physical aspects of the earth. Geoscientists study the planet's geologic past and present by using sophisticated instruments and by analyzing the composition of the earth and water. Many geoscientists are involved in searching for adequate supplies of natural resources, such as groundwater, metals, and petroleum, while others work closely with environmental and other scientists in preserving and cleaning up the environment.

Geoscientists are usually classified into one of several closely related fields. Geologists study the composition, processes, and history of the earth. They try to find out how rocks were formed and what has happened to them since their formation. They also study the evolution of life by analyzing plant and animal fossils. Geophysicists use the principles of physics, mathematics, and chemistry to study not only the earth's surface, but also its internal composition, ground and surface waters, atmosphere, and oceans, as well as its magnetic, electrical, and gravitational forces.

Geoscientists can spend a large part of their time in the field, identifying and examining rocks, studying information collected by remote-sensing instruments in satellites, conducting geological surveys, constructing field maps, and using instruments to measure the earth's gravity and magnetic field. For example, they often perform seismic studies, which involve bouncing energy waves off buried layers of rock to search for oil and gas or to understand the structure of the subsurface layers. Seismic signals generated by an earthquake are used to determine the earthquake's location and intensity.

In laboratories, geologists and geophysicists examine the chemical and physical properties of specimens. They study fossil remains of animal and plant life or experiment with the flow of water and oil through rocks.

There are numerous specialties within geology and geophysics that further differentiate the type of work geoscientists do. For example, petroleum geologists map the subsurface of the ocean or land as they explore the terrain for oil and gas deposits. They use sophisticated geophysical instrumentation and computers to interpret geological information. Engineering geologists apply geologic principles to the fields of civil and environmental engineering, offering advice on major construction projects and assisting in environmental remediation and natural-hazard-reduction projects.

Mineralogists analyze and classify minerals and precious stones according to their composition and structure. They study the environment surrounding rocks in order to find new mineral resources. Sedimentologists study the nature, origin, distribution, and alteration of sediments, such as sand, silt, and mud. These sediments may contain oil, gas, coal, and many other mineral deposits. Paleontologists study fossils found in geological formations to trace the evolution of plant and animal life and the geologic history of the earth.

Stratigraphers examine the formation and layering of rocks to understand the environment in which they were formed. Volcanologists investigate volcanoes and volcanic phenomena to try to predict the potential for future eruptions and hazards to human health and welfare. Glacial geologists study the physical properties and movement of glaciers and ice sheets.

Geochemists study the nature and distribution of chemical elements in groundwater and earth materials. Geophysicists specialize in areas such as geodesy, seismology, and magnetic geophysics. Geodesists study the earth's size, shape, gravitational field, tides, polar motion, and rotation. Seismologists interpret data from seismographs and other geophysical instruments to detect earthquakes and locate earthquake-related faults.

Geomagnetists measure the earth's magnetic field and use measurements taken over the past few centuries to devise theoretical models that explain the earth's origin. Paleomagnetists interpret fossil magnetization in rocks and sediments from the continents and oceans to record the spreading of the sea floor, the wandering of the continents, and the many reversals of polarity that the earth's magnetic field has undergone through time. Other geophysicists study atmospheric sciences and space physics.

Meteorologists

Atmospheric science is the study of the atmosphere—the blanket of air covering the earth. Atmospheric scientists, commonly called meteorologists, study the atmosphere's physical characteristics, motions, and processes and the way in which these factors affect the rest of our environment. The best-known application of this knowledge is forecasting the weather. In addition to predicting the weather, atmospheric scientists attempt to identify and interpret climate trends, understand past weather patterns, and analyze today's weather. Weather information and meteorological research are also applied in air-pollution control, agriculture, forestry, air and sea transportation, defense, and the study of possible trends in the earth's climate, such as global warming, droughts, and ozone depletion.

Atmospheric scientists who forecast the weather, known professionally as operational meteorologists, are the largest group of specialists within this field. Using data gathered from weather satellites, radars, sensors, and stations around the world, they study air pressure, temperature, humidity, and wind velocity, and they apply physical and mathematical relationships to make short-range and long-range weather forecasts.

Meteorologists use sophisticated computer models of the world's atmosphere to make long-term, short-term, and local-area forecasts. Weather forecasting has been revolutionized by more accurate instruments for measuring and observing weather conditions, as well as high-speed computers to process and analyze weather data. Using satellite data, climate theory, and sophisticated computer models of the world's atmosphere, meteorologists can more effectively interpret the results of these models to make local-area weather predictions. These forecasts inform not only the general public, but also those who need accurate weather information for both economic and safety reasons, such as the shipping, air transportation, agriculture, fishing, forestry, and utilities industries.

Some atmospheric scientists work in research. Physical meteorologists, for example, study the atmosphere's chemical and physical properties; the transmission of light, sound, and radio waves; and the transfer of energy in the atmosphere. They also study factors affecting the formation of clouds, rain, and snow; the dispersal of air pollutants over urban areas; and other weather phenomena, such as the mechanics of severe storms. Synoptic meteorologists develop new tools for weather forecasting using computers and sophisticated mathematical models of atmospheric activity. Climatologists study climactic variations spanning hundreds or even millions of years. They also may collect, analyze, and interpret past records of wind, rainfall, sunshine, and temperature in specific areas or regions. Their studies are used to design buildings, plan heating and cooling systems, and aid in effective land use and agricultural production. Environmental meteorologists study such problems as pollution and shortages of fresh water and may evaluate and report on air quality for environmental impact statements. Other research meteorologists examine the most effective ways to control or diminish air pollution.

Training for Chemists

A bachelor's degree in chemistry or a related discipline usually is the minimum educational requirement for entry-level chemist jobs. However, many research positions require a master's degree or more often a doctorate. Many colleges and universities offer degree programs in chemistry. In 2005, the American Chemical Society (ACS) approved 631 bachelor's, 308 master's, and 192 doctoral degree programs. In addition to these schools, several hundred colleges and universities also offer advanced degree programs in chemistry.

Students planning careers as chemists should take courses in science and mathematics, should like working with their hands building scientific apparatuses and performing laboratory experiments, and should understand computer modeling. Curiosity, perseverance, and the ability to concentrate on minute detail and to work independently are essential. Interaction among specialists in this field is increasing, especially for specialty chemists in drug development. Chemists in one specialty often rely on the findings of chemists in another area. For example, an organic chemist must understand findings on the identity of compounds prepared by an analytical chemist.

In addition to required courses in analytical, inorganic, organic, and physical chemistry, undergraduate chemistry majors usually study biological sciences, mathematics, physics, and, increasingly, computer science. Computer courses are essential because employers prefer job applicants who can apply computer skills to modeling and simulation tasks and can operate computerized laboratory equipment. Courses in statistics are useful because chemists need the ability to apply basic statistical techniques in data analysis.

Because R&D chemists are increasingly expected to work on interdisciplinary teams, some understanding of other disciplines, including business and marketing or economics, is desirable, along with leadership ability and good oral and written communication skills. Other useful experience includes work in academic laboratories or through internships, fellowships, or work-study programs in industry. Some employers of research chemists prefer to hire individuals with several years of postdoctoral experience; this is especially true in the pharmaceutical industry.

Graduate students typically specialize in a subfield of chemistry, such as analytical chemistry or polymer chemistry, depending on their interests and the kind of work they wish to do. For example, those who hope to work in drug research in the pharmaceutical industry usually develop a strong background in medicinal or synthetic organic chemistry. However, students normally need not specialize at the undergraduate level. In fact, undergraduates who are broadly trained have more flexibility when job hunting or changing jobs than if they have narrowly defined their interests. Most employers provide new graduates with additional training or education.

In government or industry, beginning chemists with a bachelor's degree work in quality control, perform analytical testing, or assist senior chemists in R&D laboratories. Many employers prefer chemists with a doctorate, or at least a master's degree, to lead basic and applied research. Chemists who hold a doctorate and have previous industrial experience may be particularly attractive to employers because such people are more likely to understand the complex regulations that apply to the pharmaceutical industry. Within materials science, a broad background in various sciences is preferred. This broad base may be obtained through degrees in physics, engineering, or chemistry.

Training for Physicists and Astronomers

Because most jobs are in basic research and development, a doctoral degree is the usual educational requirement for physicists and astronomers. Although it is not required, additional experience and training in a postdoctoral research appointment is important for those who aspire to permanent positions in basic research in universities and government laboratories. Many physics and astronomy Ph.D. holders ultimately teach at the college or university level.

Master's degree holders usually do not qualify for basic research positions, but they do qualify for many kinds of jobs requiring a physics background, including positions in manufacturing and applied research and development. Increasingly, many master's degree programs are specifically preparing students for physics-related research and development that does not require a doctorate. These programs teach students specific research skills that can be used in private-industry jobs. In addition, a master's degree coupled with state certification usually qualifies one for teaching jobs in high schools or at two-year colleges.

Those with bachelor's degrees in physics are rarely qualified to fill positions in research or in teaching at the college level. They are, however, usually qualified to work as technicians or research assistants in engineering-related areas, in software development, in other scientific fields, or in setting up computer networks and sophisticated laboratory equipment. Increasingly, some may qualify for applied research jobs in private industry or take on nontraditional physics roles, often in computer science, such as a systems analyst or database administrator. Some become science teachers in secondary schools.

Graduates with a bachelor's or master's degree in astronomy often enter an unrelated field. In addition, they are qualified to work in planetariums running science shows, to assist astronomers doing research, and to operate space-based and ground-based telescopes and other astronomical instrumentation.

About 510 colleges and universities offer a bachelor's degree in physics. Undergraduate programs provide a broad background in the natural sciences and mathematics. Typical physics courses include electromagnetism, optics, thermodynamics, quantum mechanics, and atomic physics. Approximately 185 colleges and universities have departments offering doctoral degrees in physics; an additional 68 colleges offer a master's as their highest degree in physics. Graduate students usually concentrate in a subfield of physics, such as elementary particles or condensed matter. Many begin studying for a doctorate immediately after receiving a bachelor's degree.

About eighty universities grant degrees in astronomy, either through an astronomy, physics, or combined physics-astronomy department. With fewer than forty doctoral programs in astronomy, applicants face considerable competition for available slots. Those planning a career in the subject should have a very strong physics background. In fact, an undergraduate degree in either physics or astronomy is excellent preparation, followed by a doctorate in astronomy.

Mathematical ability, problem-solving and analytical skills, an inquisitive mind, imagination, and initiative are important traits for anyone planning a career in physics or astronomy. Prospective physicists who hope to work in industrial laboratories applying physics knowledge to practical problems should broaden their educational background to include courses outside of physics, such as economics, information technology, and business management. Good oral and written communication skills also are important because many physicists work as part of a team, write research papers or proposals, or have contact with clients or customers without physics backgrounds.

Training for Geologists and Geophysicists

A bachelor's degree is adequate for a few entry-level positions, but most geoscientists need at least a master's degree in general geology or earth science. A master's degree also is the minimum educational requirement for most entry-level research positions in private industry, federal agencies, and state geological surveys. A doctoral degree is necessary for most high-level research and college teaching positions.

Many colleges and universities offer a bachelor's or higher degree in a geoscience. In 2005, more than one hundred universities offered accredited bachelor's degree programs in geoscience, about eighty universities had master's degree programs, and about sixty offered doctoral degree programs.

Traditional geoscience courses emphasizing classical geologic methods and topics are important for all geoscientists. Students studying physics, chemistry, biology, mathematics, engineering, or computer science may also qualify for some geoscience positions if their course work includes study in geology or natural sciences.

Computer skills are essential for prospective geoscientists; students who have experience with computer modeling, data analysis and integration, digital mapping, remote sensing, and geographic information systems will be the most prepared to enter the job market. Knowledge of the Geographic Information System (GIS) and Global Positioning System (GPS)—a locator system that uses satellites—has also become essential. Some employers seek applicants with field experience, so a summer internship may be beneficial to prospective geoscientists.

Geoscientists must have excellent interpersonal skills because they usually work as part of a team with other geoscientists and with environmental scientists, engineers, and technicians. Strong oral and written communication skills also are important because writing technical reports and research proposals, as well as communicating research results to others, are important aspects of the work. Because many jobs require foreign travel, knowledge of a second language is becoming an important attribute to employers. Geoscientists must be inquisitive, able to think logically, and capable of complex analytical thinking, including spatial visualization and the ability to develop comprehensive conclusions often from sparse data. Those involved in fieldwork must have physical stamina.

Geoscientists often begin their careers in field exploration or as research assistants or technicians in laboratories or offices. They are given more difficult assignments as they gain experience. Eventually, they may be promoted to project leader, program manager, or some other management or research position.

Training for Meteorologists

A bachelor's degree in meteorology or atmospheric science, or in a closely related field with courses in meteorology, usually is the minimum educational requirement for an entry-level position as an atmospheric scientist. The preferred educational requirement for entry-level meteorologists in the federal government is a bachelor's degree (not necessarily in meteorology) with at least twenty-four semester hours of meteorology courses, including six hours in the analysis and prediction of weather systems, six hours of atmospheric dynamics and thermodynamics, three hours of physical meteorology, and two hours of remote sensing of the atmosphere or instrumentation. Other required courses include three semester hours of ordinary differential equations, six hours of college physics, and at least nine hours of courses appropriate for a physical science major—such as statistics, chemistry, physical oceanography, physical climatology, physical hydrology, radiative transfer, aeronomy, advanced thermodynamics, advanced electricity and magnetism, light and optics, and computer science. Sometimes, a combination of education and appropriate experience may be substituted for a degree.

Although positions in operational meteorology are available for those with only a bachelor's degree, obtaining a second bachelor's degree or a master's degree enhances employment opportunities, pay, and advancement potential. A master's degree usually is necessary for conducting applied research and development, and a doctorate is required for most basic research positions. Students planning on a career in research and development do not necessarily need to major in atmospheric science or meteorology as an undergraduate. In fact, a bachelor's degree in mathematics, physics, or engineering provides excellent preparation for graduate study in atmospheric science.

Because atmospheric science is a small field, relatively few colleges and universities offer degrees in meteorology or atmospheric science, although many departments of physics, earth science, geography, and geophysics offer atmospheric science and related courses. In 2005, the American Meteorological Society (AMS) approved approximately one hundred undergraduate and graduate atmospheric science programs. Many of these programs combine the study of meteorology with another field, such as agriculture, hydrology, oceanography, engineering, or physics. For example, hydrometeorology is the blending of hydrology (the science of the earth's water) and meteorology and is the field concerned with the effect of precipitation on the hydrologic cycle and the environment.

Prospective students should make certain that courses required by the National Weather Service and other employers are offered at the college they are considering. Computer science courses, additional meteorology courses, a strong background in mathematics and physics, and good communication skills are important to prospective employers.

Students should also take courses in subjects that are most relevant to their area of specialization. For example, those who wish to become broadcast meteorologists for radio or television should develop excellent communication skills through courses in speech, journalism, and related fields. Students interested in air quality work should take courses in chemistry and supplement their technical training with course work in policy or government affairs. Prospective meteorologists seeking opportunities at weather consulting firms should possess knowledge of business, statistics, and economics, as an increasing emphasis is being placed on long-range seasonal forecasting to assist businesses.

AMS offers professional certification of consulting meteorologists, administered by a board of Certified Consulting Meteorologists. Applicants must meet formal education requirements (but not necessarily have a college degree), pass an examination to demonstrate thorough meteorological knowledge, have a minimum of five years of experience or a combination of experience plus an advanced degree, and provide character references from fellow professionals. In addition, AMS also offers professional certification for broadcast meteorologists.

Earnings for Chemists

The American Chemical Society (ACS) reports that in 2004 the median salary of all of its members with bachelor's degrees was $62,000; for those with master's degrees, it was $72,300; and for those with doctorates, it was $91,600. The median salary was highest for those working in private industry and lowest for those in academia.

According to an ACS survey of recent graduates, inexperienced chemistry graduates with bachelor's degrees earned median starting salaries of $32,500 in October 2004; those with master's degrees earned median salaries of $43,600; and those with doctorates had median earnings of $65,000. Among bachelor's degree graduates, those who had completed internships or had other work experience commanded the highest starting salaries.

In 2004, median annual earnings in the industries that employed the largest number of chemists were federal government, $80,550; scientific research and development services, $62,460; pharmaceutical and medicine manufacturing, $57,050; and architectural, engineering, and related services, $42,370.

Earnings for Physicists and Astronomers

According to a 2005 survey by the National Association of Colleges and Employers, the average annual starting salary offer to physics doctoral degree candidates was $56,070.

The American Institute of Physics reported a median annual salary of $104,000 in 2004 for its full-time members with doctorates (excluding those in postdoctoral positions); the median was $94,000 for those with master's degrees and $72,000 for bachelor's degree holders. Those working in temporary postdoctoral positions earned significantly less.

Median annual earnings of physicists were $87,450 in May 2004. Median annual earnings of astronomers were $97,320. The average annual salary for physicists employed by the federal government was $104,917 in 2005; for astronomy and space scientists, it was $110,195.

Earnings for Geologists and Geophysicists

According to the National Association of Colleges and Employers, beginning salary offers in July 2005 for graduates with bachelor's degrees in geology and related sciences averaged $39,365 a year. In 2005, the average salary for geologists in managerial, supervisory, and nonsupervisory positions with the federal government was $83,178 and $94,836 for geophysicists.

Median annual earnings of geoscientists were $68,730 in May 2004. The middle 50 percent earned between $49,260 and $98,380; the lowest 10 percent earned less than $37,700, and the highest 10 percent more than $130,750.

The petroleum, mineral, and mining industries are vulnerable to recessions and to changes in oil and gas prices, among other factors, and usually release workers when exploration and drilling slow down. Consequently, they offer higher salaries but less job security than other industries.

Earnings for Meteorologists

Median annual earnings of atmospheric scientists in May 2004 were $70,100. The middle 50 percent earned between $48,880 and $86,610. The lowest 10 percent earned less than $34,590, and the highest 10 percent earned more than $106,020.

The average salary for meteorologists in nonsupervisory, supervisory, and managerial positions employed by the federal government was about $80,499 in 2005. Meteorologists in the federal government with bachelor's degrees and no experience received a starting salary of $27,955 or $34,544, depending on their college grades.

Those with master's degrees could start at $42,090 or $54,393, and those with doctorates could begin at $70,280. Beginning salaries for all degree levels are slightly higher in areas of the country where the prevailing local pay level is higher.

Meet Some Physical Science Researchers

Following are two personal accounts by physical science researchers. Perhaps their experiences will inspire your competitive spirit.

Ken Rubin, Ph.D.

Dr. Ken Rubin serves as an associate professor on the staff of the University of Hawaii at Manoa in the Department of Geology and Geophysics, School of Ocean and Earth Science and Technology (SOEST). He earned a bachelor's degree in chemistry from the University of California at San Diego (UCSD), followed by graduate studies at UCSD's Scripps Institute of Oceanography, where he received his master's and doctoral degrees. Dr. Rubin came to the University of Hawaii as an assistant researcher; after three years he was promoted to assistant professor.

Dr. Rubin was hired by the University of Hawaii in a competitive search for a postdoctoral position known as the SOEST Young Investigator, which is a research faculty position at the assistant level that allows one to write grant proposals to federal funding agencies and to work independent of a supervisor. The positions are offered once or twice each year, and applicants are selected from a variety of disciplines, such as earth sciences, oceanography, marine biology, atmospheric sciences, and ocean engineering.

Dr. Rubin entered into an agreement with the dean and other faculty to establish a state-of-the-art thermal ionization mass spectrometry facility for analyzing radioactive isotopes. This was a significant commitment, since his position was for two years and it normally takes three to five years to fund and set up a lab of this type. However, the university agreed to extend Dr. Rubin's assistant researcher position beyond its two-year term pending significant productivity on his part. Setting up the lab required securing federal support for the purchase of a $750,000 mass spectrometer. Dr. Rubin obtained 25 percent each from the National Science Foundation Earth Sciences and Ocean Sciences Divisions and 50 percent from SOEST.

After securing the necessary funding and starting to set up the lab, Dr. Rubin was offered a position as assistant professor at the University of Miami's Rosenstiel School of Marine and Atmospheric Sciences (RSMAS). Since the economy of Hawaii was entering an economic downturn, he felt it was necessary to seek another position but hoped that the University of Hawaii would offer him a more permanent situation. In the end, an assistant professorship was approved by SOEST and the University of Hawaii. A national search was conducted to fill the position, and Dr. Rubin was selected for the job.

Although he initially wanted to be a medical doctor, during his freshman year of college Dr. Rubin became very interested in chemistry with environmental applications. At the same time, he became enamored of the academician's career and lifestyle, and he switched his career aspirations to becoming a professor at a research university. "I have nothing against private sector or government jobs," he says, "and I know I could find some level of fulfillment in pursuits there. However, it was clear to me then and still is today that the level of intellectual freedom that the university system in America affords makes this sort of job highly rewarding."

Dr. Rubin works between eight and twelve hours a day, seven days a week. One reason for this schedule is that his research requires lengthy and exacting analytical procedures that make long hours necessary. Another reason is that he enjoys his work and has taken on other duties besides research and teaching. He teaches one or two upper-division and/or graduate-level courses each semester and serves as advisor to graduate students. Dr. Rubin's lab research is done in one- to two-month intervals during which he might spend all of his time (when not teaching) in the lab, in the field, or in his office reducing data and interpreting results.

Fieldwork includes research on active volcanoes on land and on the sea floor, and almost all of the lab work involves toxic chemicals and radioactive substances. This dangerous work isn't for everyone, but Dr. Rubin finds it rewarding because of the day-to-day challenges. He says, "The part that makes it unique, and the difficult thing to pass on to students, is the application of high-precision measurements requiring exacting care and uncompromising standards to natural phenomena. Although the lab and fieldwork are both necessary aspects of the research we do, the two environments are very different and require different mind-sets."

In addition to teaching and research, Dr. Rubin has been involved in getting the school on the Internet. He developed and oversees numerous websites at the school, including interactive sites providing answers to the public to questions about science and resource sites dedicated to educating lay people and researchers about active processes at volcanoes and the latest research going on at the University of Hawaii. "I use the Internet in my courses and love what it offers," Dr. Rubin says. "Once a person relates to and accepts the way in which people make computers process and make information available, their mind is freed to cross the boundaries between the abstract and the physical. Computers are a wonderful and indispensable teaching tool."

As much as he loves his work, Dr. Rubin is honest about the reality of holding an academic research position. "To enjoy the academic and intellectual freedom, friendly atmosphere, youthful environment, and flexible hours, one must be very disciplined," he says. "This can make it difficult, as you must evaluate yourself and your progress frequently and cannot rely on infrequent or nonexistent direction from a superior. You must sense the expectations of your peers and then work to satisfy them while not sacrificing your own goals and desires. You must be self-motivated and take a very long-range perspective on success in the attainment of work-related goals."

As is the case in most academic environments, funding is an ongoing issue faced by the research scientist. Dr. Rubin describes a "lack of funds at all levels. The golden age of scientific research died out in the 1980s (if not earlier). I watch my older colleagues struggling to adapt to this new environment, but since I never knew the days of seemingly unlimited research funds, I don't get as depressed as they at the difficulty of getting research funded today.

"Jobs are very difficult to obtain, so always work hard at everything you do. Not only are top-notch resumes required to land one of these jobs, but hard work will be required to keep it. A university professor's life may appear to be genteel and rewarding and filled with healthy doses of wisdom and cups of cappuccino at the local coffeehouse, but it is actually rigorous on many levels."

Glen D. Lawrence, Ph.D.

Dr. Glen Lawrence is professor of biochemistry and bioinorganic chemistry at Long Island University, where he has worked since 1985. He received his B.S. in chemistry from Pratt Institute in Brooklyn, New York; his M.A. in chemistry from SUNY at Plattsburgh, New York; and his Ph.D. in biochemistry from Utah State University in Logan, Utah. He served as a science advisor for the U.S. Food and Drug Administration New York Regional Laboratory from 1988 to 1992, advising analytical chemists in research projects related to drug chemistry.

Dr. Lawrence first became interested in the functioning of living organisms during his childhood on a farm in rural New York. Since there were no scientists in his community, and he received little guidance in high school, he was not certain what direction to take after graduation. Aptitude in science and math led him to pursue a career in chemistry, and those studies brought out his fascination with biochemistry. He enrolled in a master's degree program in a chemistry department, with a biochemist as his research advisor. After completing his graduate studies, Dr. Lawrence realized that he wanted to pursue a career in academia and went on to earn his Ph.D. in biochemistry.

With a long-standing interest in conservation, Dr. Lawrence applied for a research fellowship to study model systems for photosynthesis, wanting to study the development of materials that could be used to convert solar energy into useful chemical energy. The project was aimed at developing materials that would utilize light to catalyze the splitting of water into hydrogen and oxygen, which could later be used as fuels. Dr. Lawrence studied the problem for a year in West Germany, where he realized the difficulty of accomplishing his goal. He had the opportunity to spend several years conducting research at different laboratories, an experience that he calls extremely valuable in broadening his general knowledge of science and his specific knowledge of biochemistry, pharmacology, physiology, and toxicology.

In 1985, when funding for his research project was ending, Dr. Lawrence accepted a position at Long Island University in the master's degree program in chemistry. "Although I was planning to hold out for a faculty position at a research institution," he says, "the master's degree program at the LIU Brooklyn campus provided ample opportunity for research, along with interesting possibilities for teaching advanced courses in special areas, such as neurochemistry and advanced analytical techniques for biomedical analysis."

Dr. Lawrence teaches nine hours of courses per week, including such classes as introductory chemistry for nonscience majors; chemistry for the health sciences; biochemistry for chemistry and molecular biology majors; and graduate courses in analytical chemistry, biochemistry, and neurochemistry. He occasionally teaches an elective course for honors students. In addition to teaching, Dr. Lawrence serves as advisor to undergraduate and graduate students working on research projects.

Dr. Lawrence and his students work in a small lab. While their work itself is not dangerous, they nevertheless must take precautions when performing some experiments. The materials they work with are not generally explosive or toxic, but they must be aware of any that are and handle them in the proper fashion.

As a professor, Dr. Lawrence also serves on various campus committees. Though these committees vary from year to year, all take up a substantial amount of time. The committee work may include the evaluation of junior faculty members for promotion and tenure, discussion of new courses and curricula that are being proposed for the university, review of existing courses and programs and the regular reevaluation of the campus for accreditation, or attention to the day-to-day running of the university.

Dr. Lawrence is also frequently asked to review a master's degree candidate's thesis to determine whether the student meets the department's approval to obtain a degree. When he is the student's advisor, this usually requires advising the candidate about how to write a master's thesis and reading the thesis many times to suggest all the necessary corrections before it is submitted to the student's committee. This all occurs after guiding the student through a research project that usually lasts about a year and involves developing methods for analyzing certain chemicals, collecting a wealth of data to support a hypothesis, analyzing the data to see if it supports the hypothesis, and finally deciding how to present the data so it will be understandable to others who may be interested.

During the years that he served as science advisor to the Food and Drug Administration (FDA), Dr. Lawrence visited the FDA labs once a week to discuss research projects with the analytical chemists who worked to analyze drugs being sold by pharmaceutical companies. The FDA must use well-established methods for drug analysis that have undergone extensive testing in both the FDA labs as well as the pharmaceutical manufacturers' labs. Some of these methods rely on procedures that may be many years old, but newer methods could save much time without sacrificing accuracy. However, any new method must be tested before it can become an established method in their protocol.

Dr. Lawrence's job was to work with the FDA chemists in an attempt to streamline the methods used to accomplish efficient and accurate drug analysis. An example of this involved an analysis for the Department of Defense of the drugs in nerve gas antidotes. When the Persian Gulf War began, nerve gas antidotes had to be taken from storage and tested quickly to determine their suitability for use, since much of the stockpile had passed the expiration date. The existing method required forty-five minutes per sample for testing. Dr. Lawrence tried a different method that decreased the analysis time to ten minutes, which is a significant savings in time when thousands of samples must be tested. Once the new method was thoroughly tested, it was found to be very suitable for military samples as well as for a wide variety of dosage forms, including eye drops and some other medications.

Dr. Lawrence finds a lot of satisfaction in his career. "Whether in the classroom or the laboratory, teaching can be very exciting," he says. "Other times it can be extremely frustrating. Sometimes students show a genuine interest in the material; other times I get a whole classroom of students who just don't want to be there, but it is a requirement for them to graduate. Many come into the class dreading it initially but find after a while that we are covering things that can be quite interesting, such as the greenhouse effect, global warming, air and water pollution, destruction of the ozone layer, and guidelines about how to keep your body healthy. By the time the students get finished, some of them realize that it was a worthwhile college experience.

"Probably the most rewarding aspect of my job is realized when a student decides to do a special project, either in the form of research in the lab or a library research project, and that student begins to comprehend the complexities of science, especially the life sciences. If I feel that I could instill in another individual the desire to pursue a career in science or just to understand more about how the world works on the molecular level, then I feel I have accomplished my goal. Even if only a handful of my students realize this in my lifetime, I will have passed something on to the next generation."

For More Information

Additional information about the careers detailed in this chapter is available from several sources.

Biological and Medical Sciences
For information on careers in physiology, contact:

American Physiological Society (APS)
Membership Services Department
9650 Rockville Pike
Bethesda, MD 20814
www.the-aps.org

For information on careers in biotechnology, contact:

Biotechnology Industry Organization (BIO)
1225 I Street NW, Suite 400
Washington, DC 20005
www.bio.org

For information on careers in biochemistry, contact:

American Society for Biochemistry and Molecular Biology
    (ASBMB)
9650 Rockville Pike
Bethesda, MD 20814
www.asbmb.org

For information on careers in botany, contact:

Botanical Society of America
PO Box 299
St. Louis, MO 63166
www.botany.org

For information on careers in microbiology, contact:

American Society for Microbiology (ASM)
1725 N Street NW
Washington, DC 20036
www.asm.org

Information on federal job opportunities in scientific research is available from local offices of state employment services and from the United States Office of Personnel Management. Visit the government website at www.usajobs.com.

Physical Sciences

General information on career opportunities and earnings for chemists is available from:

American Chemical Society (ACS)
1155 Sixteenth Street NW
Washington, DC 20036
www.chemistry.org

General information on career opportunities in physics is available from:

American Institute of Physics (AIP)
One Physics Ellipse
College Park, MD 20740
www.aip.org

American Physical Society (APS)
One Physics Ellipse
College Park, MD 20740
www.aps.org

For information on careers in astronomy, send your request to:

American Astronomical Society (AAS)
2000 Florida Avenue NW, Suite 400
Washington, DC 20009
www.aas.org

Information on training and career opportunities for geologists
is available from:

American Geological Institute (AGI)
4220 King Street
Alexandria, VA 22302
www.agiweb.org

Geological Society of America (GSA)
PO Box 9140
Boulder, CO 80301
www.geosociety.org

American Association of Petroleum Geologists (AAPG)
1444 South Boulder
Tulsa, OK 74119
www.aapg.org

Information on training and career opportunities for geophysicists is available from:

American Geophysical Union (AGU)
2000 Florida Avenue NW
Washington, DC 20009
www.agu.org

A list of curricula in colleges and universities offering programs in oceanography and related fields is available from:

Marine Technology Society (MTS)
5565 Sterrett Place, Suite 108
Columbia, MD 21044
www.mtsociety.org

Information on career opportunities in meteorology is available from:

American Meteorological Society (AMS)
45 Beacon Street
Boston, MA 02108
www.ametsoc.org

National Oceanic and Atmospheric Administration (NOAA)
Fourteenth Street & Constitution Avenue NW, Room 6217
Washington, DC 20230
www.noaa.gov

Information on federal job opportunities in the physical sciences is available from local offices of state employment services and from the United States Office of Personnel Management. Visit the website at www.usajobs.com.

CHAPTER SIX

Careers in Entertainment

*Acting is the most minor of gifts. After all,
Shirley Temple could do it when she was four.*
—Katharine Hepburn

Perhaps you've been entertaining your family since childhood, staging plays in the living room wearing your parents' clothes. Maybe you were the class clown, making classmates (and even teachers) laugh at your jokes and antics. You probably auditioned for every production your school staged—and usually won a starring role. If this sounds like you, then a career in the world of entertainment just might be for you.

Welcome to the World of Acting

Whether portraying someone young or old, dramatic or comedic, actors bring their characters to life using voices, gestures, and movements. Actors perform in stage, radio, television, video, or motion-picture productions. They also work in cabarets, nightclubs, theme parks, commercials, and industrial films produced for training and educational purposes.

Though acting is often viewed as a glamorous profession, the truth is that many actors are forced to put in long and irregular hours (including rehearsals and performances) with little payment in return. Most actors struggle to find steady work; only a few ever achieve recognition as stars. Some well-known, experienced performers may be cast in supporting roles. Others work as "extras," with no lines to deliver, or make brief, cameo appearances, speaking only one or two lines. Some actors do voiceover and narration work for advertisements, animated features, books on tape, and other electronic media. They also teach in high school or university drama departments, acting conservatories, or public programs.

Training for Actors

Experienced actors recommend that those who hope to pursue this career gain experience by taking part in high school and college productions. In addition, performing in local community theater also provides an opportunity for aspiring actors to hone their skills. Public high schools dedicated to education in the performing arts can be found in many cities throughout the United States and Canada.

Formal dramatic training, either through an acting conservatory or a university program, generally is necessary to enter the profession; however, some people successfully enter the field without it. Most people studying for a bachelor's degree take courses in radio and television broadcasting, communications, film, theater, drama, or dramatic literature. Many continue their academic training and receive a master of fine arts (M.F.A.) degree. Advanced curricula may include courses in stage speech and movement, directing, playwriting, and design, as well as intensive acting workshops. The National Association of Schools of Theatre accredits 128 programs in theater arts.

Many actors, regardless of experience level, pursue continued training through acting conservatories or by working with a drama coach. Actors also research roles so that they can grasp concepts quickly during rehearsals and understand the story's setting and background. Sometimes actors learn a foreign language or train with a dialect coach to develop an accent to make their characters more realistic.

Desirable Qualities

Among the most desirable personal traits for actors are creative instincts, innate talent, and the intellectual ability to perform. Actors should be passionate about performing and truly enjoy entertaining others. In addition, determination, perseverance, and a good memory also enhance an actor's ability to win roles.

Actors must have poise, stage presence, and the ability to affect an audience. They must also be able to follow direction. Since physical appearance can definitely be a deciding factor in being selected for particular roles, actors should be able and willing to adopt different looks when pursuing new roles. Actors also need stamina to withstand the heat of stage or studio lights, heavy costumes, the irregular hours, and the adverse weather conditions that may exist when working on location.

Building a Career

The best way to start building an acting career is to pursue local opportunities and move on from there to larger prospects. Basic experience can be acquired through modeling, acting groups, and local and regional theater. Any or all of these may help in obtaining work in the major entertainment markets—New York and Los Angeles.

Most actors list themselves with casting agencies that help them find parts. Many also take advantage of the services offered by the unions listed at the end of this chapter. Many professional actors rely on agents or managers to find work, negotiate contracts, and plan their careers. Agents generally earn a percentage of an actor's contract.

As actors' reputations grow, they work on larger productions or in more prestigious theaters. Actors also advance to lead or specialized roles. A few actors move into acting-related jobs as drama coaches or directors of stage, television, radio, or motion-picture productions. Some teach drama in colleges and universities.

The length of a performer's working life depends largely on training, skill, versatility, and perseverance. Some actors continue working throughout their lives; however, large numbers also leave the occupation after a short time because they cannot find enough work to make a living.

Extra! Extra! Read All About It!

In addition to actors with speaking parts, extras are widely used throughout the industry. An extra is an actor who has a small role with no lines to deliver. To become a movie extra (also known as a background artist), one must usually be listed by a casting agency, such as Central Casting, a no-fee agency that supplies extras to the major movie studios in Hollywood.

Acting Strategies—Finding a Job

Armed with your college degree, basic knowledge of the acting business, and some experience, you'll need to prepare a portfolio that highlights your qualifications, acting history, and special skills. This will take the form of a resume along with photos, or "head shots," taken by a professional photographer whom you trust to show you off to your best advantage. Attach your resume to the back of your picture with staples at the upper left and right corners.

Once your portfolio is complete, you can start making the rounds of casting offices, ad agencies, producers' offices, and agents. Several trade publications contain casting information, ads for part-time jobs, information about shows, and other pertinent data about what's going on in the industry. Among these are *Back Stage* and the weekly *Variety* in New York and Los Angeles, and *Ross Reports* in New York. In Los Angeles, there's also *Daily Variety* and *Hollywood Reporter*. You can find all of these, as well as other information about casting calls and acting opportunities, on the Internet.

Once you drop off your resume and head shots, you certainly shouldn't just wait for the phone to ring. Stay active by remaining in contact—it may even be a good idea to drop by the various offices and say hello. Be sure to check in by phone every week to see if any opportunities are available for you. If you are currently in a show, send prospective employers a flyer. This shows them that you are a working actor.

When you get past this initial stage and actually win an audition, here are some things you should remember:

1. Be prepared.
2. Be familiar with the piece—read it beforehand and choose the parts you'd like to try out for.
3. Go for it—don't hold back.
4. Speak loudly and clearly—project to the back of the room.
5. Take chances.
6. Try not to be the one going first—if you can. Observe others so that you can pick up on what the evaluators seem to like or dislike.
7. Be enthusiastic and confident.
8. Keep auditioning—even if you don't get parts, you are getting invaluable experience that is bound to pay off at some point.

So, when should you get an agent? The answer is, not right away. You don't need an agent to audition for everything, and there are many roles you can audition for that do not require an agent, such as theater or films. However, most commercials are cast through agencies, so you would most likely need an agent to land one.

Earnings for Actors

Minimum salaries, hours of work, and other conditions of employment are covered in collective bargaining agreements between producers of shows and unions representing workers in this field. The Actors' Equity Association represents stage actors; the Screen Actors Guild (SAG) and the Screen Extras Guild cover actors in motion pictures, including television, commercials, and films; and the American Federation of Television and Radio Artists (AFTRA) represents performers in television and radio. Some actors who regularly work in several media find it advantageous to join multiple unions, while SAG and AFTRA may share jurisdiction for work in additional areas, such as the production of training or educational films not slated for broadcast, television commercial work, and interactive media. While these unions generally determine minimum salaries, any actor or director may negotiate for a salary higher than the minimum.

Under terms of a joint SAG and AFTRA contract covering all unionized workers, motion picture and television actors with speaking parts earned a minimum daily rate of $716 or $2,483 for a five-day week, as of October 1, 2005. Actors also receive contributions to their health and pension plans and additional compensation for reruns and foreign telecasts of the productions in which they appear.

According to Equity, the minimum weekly salary for actors in Broadway productions as of June 30, 2005, was $1,422. Actors in off-Broadway theaters received minimums ranging from $493 to $857 a week as of October 23, 2005, depending on the seating capacity of the theater. Regional theaters that operate under an Equity agreement pay actors $531 to $800 per week. For touring productions, actors receive an additional $777 per week for living expenses ($819 per week in higher-cost cities). New terms were negotiated under an "experimental touring program" provision for lower-budget musicals that tour to smaller cities or that perform for fewer performances at each stop. In an effort to increase the number of paid workweeks while on tour, actors may be paid less than the full production rate for touring shows in exchange for higher per diems and profit participation.

Some well-known actors earn well above the minimum; their salaries are many times the figures cited, creating the false impression that all actors are highly paid. For example, of the nearly a hundred thousand SAG members, only about fifty might be considered stars. The average income that SAG members earn from acting—less than $5,000 a year—is low because employment is sporadic. Most actors must supplement their incomes by holding jobs in other occupations.

Many actors who work more than a qualifying number of days or weeks per year or earn over a set minimum pay are covered by a union health, welfare, and pension fund, which includes hospitalization insurance to which employers contribute. Under some employment conditions, Equity and AFTRA members receive paid vacations and sick leave.

Meet Some Professional Actors

Following are the personal accounts of five actors. Do their work experiences appeal to your competitive spirit?

Jennifer Aquino, Actor

Jennifer Aquino has appeared in television, movies, and stage productions. Her credits include the television shows "Without a Trace," "Weird Science," "Caroline in the City," "JAG," and "Twin Peaks." Jennifer's movie credits include *Only the Brave, Ten Thousand Years, The Party Crashers, Prisoners of Love, Screenland Drive,* and *Ralph the Waiter*. She has performed on stage in *People Like Me* at the Playwrights' Arena; *Gila River* at Japan America Theater; and *Cabaret* and *Sophisticated Barflies* at East West Players. These are only a few of her accomplishments in all three media.

Jennifer is the lead voice of Catherine Stanfield in Microsoft and Genki's Xbox car-chasing combat game *Maximum Chase* and is the recurring voice of Chelsea in the new Rugrats animated series "All Grown Up." You can also see her in a national commercial for Home Depot.

Jennifer loved performing for her family as a child and acted for the first time in elementary school. She received the Performing

Arts Award in high school and ultimately studied theater and dance at UCLA while earning a B.A. in economics. Her first break after graduation was playing Eolani in the television series "Twin Peaks," a job she won after her very first audition. Jennifer then got an agent and joined the Screen Actors Guild. She continues performing in theatrical productions and is a founding member of Theater West and the East West Players.

Like most actors starting their careers, Jennifer initially held a full-time job while pursuing her dream. She worked in the health care industry for Kaiser Foundation Health Plan and then as a health care consultant for the accounting firm Deloitte & Touche. Jennifer was fortunate since, as she says, "I was such a good employee that my managers would be flexible and let me go out on auditions. After a few years, I realized that I was working too many hours (seventy to eighty per week), and I finally had to make a decision to quit my day job and focus 100 percent of my time toward acting. After booking a few jobs, including a national commercial, I was able to do so. It was a big risk, but one I felt necessary to take. I remember what my acting coach would say— 'part-time work gets part-time results.' The more I put into acting, the more I got out of it."

As a full-time actor, Jennifer still maintains a very busy schedule. She works forty to sixty hours each week, either preparing for an upcoming job or audition or interacting with agents and managers and promoting herself to casting directors, producers, and writers. Jennifer is aware of the potential stress that can result from such a busy schedule, so she works hard at maintaining her health and having some time to relax.

Jennifer talks about the ups and downs of acting: "What I like most about my work is that I can say that I am making a living doing what I absolutely love to do and that I am pursuing my passion in life. Not too many people in this world can say that. What I like least about my work is that there are a lot of politics in it. It's not always the best actor who gets the job. Some of the time, it's a certain look, what your credits are, who you know, and so on, that determines who gets the job. There are a lot of things that are out of your control. That's just part of the business, and you have to accept it."

Gonzo Schexnayder, Actor

Gonzo Schexnayder is an actor following a different path from Jennifer's. He has a B.A. in journalism and advertising from Louisiana State University in Baton Rouge and has taken acting classes at LSU and Monterey Peninsula College in Monterey, California. In addition, he has attended Chicago's Second City Training Center and the Actors Center and is a member of both SAG and AFTRA.

Gonzo's initial dream was to do stand-up comedy, but he did not pursue it until he graduated from college and began working with an improvisational comedy group. Within a few months he was on military assignment in Monterey, California, for language training.

It was in Monterey that Gonzo had his first show, and he still recalls how happy the experience made him. "I'd never felt such elation as when I performed. Nothing in my life had given me the sheer thrill and rush that I experienced by creating a character and maintaining that throughout a given period of time. Nothing else mattered but that moment on stage, my other actors, and the scene we were performing."

Realizing how important it was for him to be happy with his work, Gonzo decided to pursue acting as his career. Although this meant working on his acting while also working at a more steady job, Gonzo was willing to make the commitment. As he says, "Sure, I'd love to have an apartment with central air and a balcony. I'd love to have a car that is still under warranty. But I know that by putting my efforts and money into my acting career, those other things don't matter. . . . Cars and apartments don't give me the satisfaction that being an actor does."

Gonzo's schedule varies depending on the project he is involved in. He is a founding member of Broad Shoulders Theatre in Chicago, which takes a good deal of his time. He is also pursuing a voice-over and on-camera career and attends classes and workshops toward that end.

Gonzo offers his views on the ups and downs of acting: "I love the process of acting and sometimes just the fast-paced, eclectic nature of the business. There is always something new to learn and something new to try. The sheer excitement of performing live is amazing, and the personal satisfaction of getting an audience to laugh or cry simply by your words and actions is very gratifying.

"I dislike pretentious actors and people who take advantage of an actor's desire to perform. As one of the only professions where there is an abundance of people willing to work for nothing, producers, casting directors, agents, and managers who only care about the money will take advantage of and abuse actors for personal gain. Being an astute actor helps prevent much of this, but one must always be on the lookout."

Jack Stauffer, Actor

Jack Stauffer, a graduate of Northwestern University, has been a working actor since 1968. He created the role of Chuck Tyler in the popular television daytime drama "All My Children" and kept that role for three and a half years—a total of 386 episodes. Other regular television appearances include "Battlestar Galactica" and "The Young and the Restless." Episodic television appearances include "Lois and Clark," "Viper," "Designing Women," "Quantum Leap," "Perfect Strangers," "Growing Pains," "Knots Landing," and "Dynasty." In all, he has appeared in forty prime-time television shows and numerous movies-of-the-week and miniseries. He was also costar of the movie *Chattanooga Choo Choo*.

In theater, he had parts in *My Fair Lady* and *Oliver* at the Grove Theatre in San Bernadino County. Other play productions include *The Music Man, Annie Get Your Gun, Fiorello, Can Can, Mister*

Roberts, and *Guys and Dolls*. His list of achievements also includes parts in more than two hundred commercials.

"I started as a child actor but really didn't become a professional until I graduated from college in 1968," says Stauffer. "I simply sold my car, moved to New York, and hit the pavement!"

Jack basically grew up in the entertainment industry. His mother worked for Warner Brothers and was W. C. Fields' radio producer. His father also worked as a radio producer and started an advertising agency that was responsible for many early television shows. Jack was accustomed to being around celebrities, and he had wanted to join the ranks of performers since he was a child.

Jack is honest about the reality of working as an actor. "Unless you are on a series or are a celebrity," he says, "you are constantly battling the belief that you will probably never work again. Thus, your workday consists of looking everywhere and calling anyone who might give you a job. Once you have done all you can do, you inevitably wait for the phone to ring. The vast majority of the time, it doesn't. So, most actors have other jobs—temporary work or selling or, in my case, teaching tennis—anything to make enough money to pay the bills so you can pursue your craft. When you are finally hired for a day or a week or a month or whatever it might be, every moment in your day suddenly has purpose. You get to do what you were meant to do, even if it is only for a short time or if the part is minuscule. You are on top of the world. Then it is over, and it is back to square one."

For Jack, the work is its own reward, and he believes that this feeling is shared by most actors who are dedicated to their craft. "The best thing about your work is the work itself," he says. "An actor lives by his emotions and his ability to convey them to an audience. A good actor makes it look easy even though it is very hard. This partially explains why so many actors are willing to work for free. It is the work that fulfills them. Of course, if you get paid, it is much better. The recognition factor is important also. That is why so many actors return to the stage. The gratification is immediate. Any actor who says the applause means nothing to him is probably lying."

Jack also discusses the negative side of his profession. "The worst thing about the industry is that absolute lack of tenure. You are only as good as your next job. Your history, experience, and so forth don't mean much. This is because there is no studio system anymore. With no continuity, it is difficult to slowly work your way up the ladder of success. The easiest way to get hired today is to have the executive producer of a hit show as your brother-in-law."

Jack Stauffer offers some candid advice for anyone considering a career in acting. "If you have an absolute, undying, uncontrollable passion to do this—and I mean you will die if you don't—then by all means, give it everything you've got. But if you are the slightest bit timid or unsure, choose another career. This is a business based on rejection, and it can destroy you. If you sell cars and somebody doesn't buy one, they simply don't want that car. As an actor, when you are turned down, they don't want you. It's difficult not to take it personally. You have to be very strong to keep at it."

Joseph Bowman, Actor

Joseph Bowman is an actor in Los Angeles who considers himself at the beginning stage of his career. A high school graduate, he has some college, vocational, and military training and has also participated in the Vanguard Theatre Ensemble Training program.

While it might seem like an unlikely background for an actor, six years in the Marine Corps actually reinforced Joseph's love of performing. "I thoroughly loved the United States military," he says. "It tended to reward a person who acted as if he enjoyed this kind of life, and I was such a person. It seems that I have always been able to act appropriately in any given situation. Older people usually find me charming. Younger people usually find me cool. I love to be the chameleon."

Following his military service, Joseph took part in a model/talent showcase. Although the production itself was not a great success, the experience rekindled his love of performing.

Joseph currently does what he calls background work. His military experience gets him work in productions that want people with actual experience for certain roles. Much of this work involves firing military weapons (blanks) and an awareness of related safety issues.

In describing his job, Joseph says, "There are not many typical days in acting because every production is very different. It is like working for a different company in a different capacity every day. I may be asked to simply put on a costume and chat (mime) with another actor for eight hours one day. Another day, I might be asked to put on the full battle dress uniform of a branch of the military and fire an M-16 at a monster that isn't there! It varies widely, and that is why I love it.

"The hours and working conditions also vary greatly. Typically, jobs consist of ten-hour days with pleasant working conditions. Sometimes a shoot can be as quick as three hours, and sometimes it takes thirteen! It all depends on what the director is looking for and when he or she sees it."

Joseph greatly enjoys being involved in the arts and having the opportunity to interact with other artists. "I most enjoy the variety and the opportunity to become a character," he says. "I have worked my share of day jobs, and I hated the monotony of them. Fame is not my goal. Riches are not my goal. I simply want to do what I love and get paid for it. That is my dream.

Joseph also realizes there are some downsides of the acting business. "The only thing I don't like about acting is that there is a lot of classism. If you are on a shoot as a background actor, many do not afford you the level of treatment that featured or lead actors enjoy. It is simply a fact of life. Most actors at a high level do not act snobbish to the lowest-rung actors, but many of the production people do."

Joseph Bowman offers some practical advice about preparing for an acting career. "I would advise those interested in this field to study the craft and art of acting as if your life depended upon it. Enjoy life and experience it to the fullest because good artists bring all their life experiences to their art. And don't let anyone tell you that you are a fool for following your dream. In your later years, would you rather look back and say, 'I wish I had at least tried' or 'I gave it my best shot, and had fun along the way'?"

Joe Hansard, Actor and Stand-Up Comedian

Auditioning for a television commercial at the age of five was enough for Joe Hansard to become hooked, and he currently works as an actor and a stand-up comedian in New York City. He attended trade school at the Broadcasting Institute of Maryland and has also been an actor in residence at the International Film & Television Workshops. Other training includes Stand-Up New York (comedian school) and the Mike Fenton Scene Study Workshop for Film. He has performed his comedy routine at several comedy clubs in New York, and his favorite acting credit is the part of Jimmy Lee Shields in the pilot episode of NBC's "Homicide."

Joe's feature film credits include *Brainiac*, *Thread*, *Soulmates*, and *The Hitter*. He has also had lead or featured roles in nearly twenty independent short films and has appeared in several corporate videos.

"I've always had a fascination for the motion-picture industry," Joe says. "I enjoy the camaraderie and collaboration that comes with a film or television project, as well as the challenges. I liken it to being in a football game, where you are given the ball and you run with it. As an actor, I try to expand on the ideas given me by bringing my own uniqueness to a role.

"Since there is nothing better than working with folks who truly love their work and get excited about what they do, I like surrounding myself with creative, enthusiastic, and energetic people. As a stand-up comedian, nothing is more exhilarating than laughter and applause. It is sweeter than any candy, and it doesn't rot my teeth!"

Joe credits his parents with supporting his aspirations. He performed at talent shows in elementary school and began doing magic tricks in his early teens. After high school, he was uncertain about his career plans, and his mother suggested a trade school for broadcasting. Joe's first job was as a DJ for an AM radio station in Shippensburg, Pennsylvania. He eventually joined SAG when director Christopher Leitch cast him in a principal role in the feature film *The Hitter*, starring Ron O'Neal and Adolph Caesar.

Establishing an acting career can be very difficult, and Joe is honest about his early struggles. "I moved to Los Angeles in the early 1980s and had an absolutely horrible experience there," he says. "I couldn't get work, had my car repossessed, went bankrupt, and was in poor shape emotionally. It was the darkest time of my life, and there seemed to be no light at the end of the tunnel. But I finally got my act together and moved back east, and that's when Barry Levinson cast me in the pilot episode of 'Homicide' on NBC. The 'Gone for Goode' episode in which I appear aired after the Super Bowl in 1993 and was the highest-rated 'Homicide' episode ever."

Following this break, Joe decided to pursue stand-up comedy as a way of getting exposure. He was a finalist in HBO's Aspen Comedy Festival 2000 northeast regional competition at the Improv. He has also performed at Caroline's, Gotham Comedy Club, Don't Tell Mama, and Stand-Up New York in New York; Atlantis Theater in Toronto; the Improv, Headliners Comedy Club, the Fun Factory, Lewie's, Champions, Wiseacres, and Winchesters in D.C. and Baltimore; and the Comedy Store in Hollywood.

Like most actors, Joe spends a good deal of time looking for work. He tracks casting leads through personal contacts with industry professionals, on the Internet, or through word of mouth. "This is a crazy business," Joe says. "Sometimes it's busy and full beyond belief and there's barely time to catch my breath.

At other times, weeks and even months go by with nary a job in sight."

Joe's schedule when he is filming a movie or television show generally consists of long days, between ten and fourteen hours. While the work is usually enjoyable, the potential exists for less than pleasant conditions. As Joe says, "There is either a real camaraderie that forms on a set or a real paranoia, depending on any number of circumstances and variables in or out of your control that are inherent to the industry. In most cases, it is quite enjoyable, as cast and crew are very professional, and you, more often than not, will get kudos when the director or producer likes the work you are doing. I've found that the entire production and creative team literally evolves into a family.

"I like to work. I love meeting and working with creative, talented actors and directors. I love the business and wouldn't trade it for anything. But the thing I like least is not having any work, having to sit idle. In any case, I see an acting coach once a week and take classes to stay tuned up."

Joe Hansard has a suggestion for aspiring actors. "I would tell others that the most important thing is to love your work. Know that there is much competition and some lean times, but always remember to enjoy what you do and have fun doing it!"

Musicians

Arthur Rubinstein learned the names of the piano keys by the time he was two years old. Ray Charles began to play the piano at age three. Yehudi Menuhin performed solos with the San Francisco Symphony Orchestra at the age of seven. Buddy Holly won five dollars singing "Down the River of Memories" at a talent show at age five. Gladys Knight won two thousand dollars singing on "Ted Mack's Amateur Hour" at age seven. Marvin Hamlisch was accepted at the Juilliard School of Music at age seven. All of these musical geniuses got their starts very early, as those who choose careers in music and dance often do.

About 249,000 musicians perform in the United States. Included in this number are those who play in any one of thirty-nine regional, ninety metropolitan, or thirty major symphony orchestras. (Large orchestras employ from eighty-five to more than a hundred musicians, while smaller ones employ sixty to seventy-five players.) Also counted are those who perform with small orchestras, symphony orchestras, and pop and jazz groups, as well as those who broadcast or record.

Instrumental musicians may play a variety of musical instruments in an orchestra, popular band, marching band, military band, concert band, symphony, dance band, rock group, or jazz group and may specialize in string, brass, woodwind, or percussion instruments or electronic synthesizers. A large percentage of musicians are proficient in playing several related instruments, such as the flute and clarinet, which increases their employment opportunities. Some who are very talented have the option to perform as soloists.

Rehearsing and performing take up much of the musicians' time and energy. In addition, musicians, especially those without agents, may need to perform a number of other routine tasks, such as making reservations, keeping track of auditions and/or recordings, arranging for sound-effects amplifiers and other equipment to enhance performances, designing lighting or costuming, doing makeup, handling bookkeeping, and setting up advertising, concerts, tickets, programs, and contracts. Musicians also need to plan the sequence of the numbers to be performed and/or arrange their music according to the conductor's instructions before performances.

Musicians must also keep their instruments clean, polished, tuned, and in proper working order. In addition, they are expected to attend meetings with agents, employers, and conductors or directors to discuss contracts, engagements, and any other business activities.

Career Opportunities

Performing musicians encompass a wide variety of careers. Here are just a few of the possibilities for musicians and others who love music but may not play an instrument.

Session Musician. The session musician is the one responsible for playing background music in a studio while a recording artist is singing. Also called freelance musicians, backup musicians, session players, or studio musicians, session musicians are used for all kinds of recordings—Broadway musicals, operas, rock and folk songs, and pop tunes.

Versatility is the most important ingredient for these professionals. The more instruments they have mastered, the greater the number of musical styles they can offer, the more possibilities for musical assignments.

Session musicians often are listed through contractors who call upon them when the need arises. Other possibilities exist through direct requests made by the artists themselves, the group members, or the management team.

The ability to sight-read is important for all musicians, but it is particularly critical for session musicians. Rehearsal time is usually very limited, and costs make it too expensive to have to do retakes.

Section Member. Section members are the individuals who play instruments in an orchestra. They must be talented at playing their instruments and able to learn the music on their own. Rehearsals are strictly designed for putting all of the instruments and individuals together and for establishing cues such as phrasing and correct breathing. It is expected that all musicians practice sufficiently on their own before rehearsals.

Concertmaster. Those chosen to be concertmasters have the important responsibility of leading the string sections of the orchestras during both rehearsals and concerts. In addition, these individuals are responsible for tuning the rest of the orchestra. This is the "music" you hear for about fifteen to twenty seconds before the musicians begin to play the first piece. Concertmasters must possess leadership abilities and be very knowledgeable about both the music and all the instruments. They answer directly to the conductor.

Floor Show Band Member. Musicians who belong to bands that perform floor shows appear in hotels, nightclubs, cruise ships, bars, concert arenas, and cafés. Usually the bands do two shows per night with a particular number of sets in each show. Additionally, they may be required to play one or two dance sets during the course of the engagement. The audience is seated during the shows and gets up to dance during the dance sets. Shows may include costumes, dialogue, singing, jokes, skits, unusual sound effects, and anything else the band decides to include. Floor show bands may be contracted to appear in one place for one night or several weeks at a time. As expected, a lot of traveling is involved for those who take up this career.

Conductor and Choral Director. The music conductor is the director for all of the performers in a musical presentation, whether it be singing or instrumental. Though there are many types of conductors—symphony, choral, dance band, opera, marching band, and ballet—in all cases the music conductor is the one in charge of interpreting the music.

Conductors audition and select musicians, choose the music to accommodate the talents and abilities of the musicians, and direct rehearsals and performances, applying conducting techniques to achieve desired musical effects such as harmony, rhythm, tempo, and shading. Orchestral conductors lead instrumental music groups, such as orchestras, dance bands, and various popular ensembles. Choral directors are in charge of choirs and glee clubs, sometimes working with a band or orchestra conductor.

Training for Musicians

Many people who become professional musicians begin studying an instrument at an early age. They may gain valuable experience playing in a school or community band or orchestra or with a group of friends. Singers usually start training when their voices mature. Participation in school musicals or choirs often provides good early training and experience.

Musicians need extensive and prolonged training to acquire the necessary skills, knowledge, and ability to interpret music. This training may be obtained through private study with an accomplished musician, in a college or university music program, in a music conservatory, or through practice with a group. For study in an institution, an audition frequently is necessary. Formal courses include musical theory, music interpretation, composition, conducting, and instrumental and voice instruction. Composers, conductors, and arrangers need advanced training in these subjects as well.

Many colleges, universities, and music conservatories grant bachelor's or higher degrees in music. Many also grant degrees in music education to qualify graduates for a state certificate to teach music in an elementary or secondary school.

Those who perform popular music must have an understanding of, and feeling for, the style of music that interests them, but classical training can expand their employment opportunities as well as their musical abilities.

Although voice training is an asset for singers of popular music, many with untrained voices have had highly successful careers. As a rule, musicians take lessons with private teachers when young and seize every opportunity to make amateur or professional appearances.

Desirable Personal Qualities

Young people who are considering careers in music should have musical talent, versatility, creative ability, poise, and the confidence and stage presence to face large audiences. Since quality performance requires constant study and practice, self-discipline is vital.

Moreover, musicians who play concert and nightclub engagements must have physical stamina because frequent travel and night performances are required. They must also be prepared to face the anxiety of intermittent employment and rejections when auditioning for work.

Earnings for Musicians

Earnings for musicians often depend on a performer's professional reputation and place of employment and on the number of hours worked. The most successful musicians can earn far more than the average minimum salaries specified by the unions. Yearly earnings typically reflect the number of gigs a freelance musician or singer played or the number of hours and weeks of salaried contract work, in addition to a performer's professional reputation and setting: performers who can fill large concert halls, arenas, or outdoor stadiums generally command higher pay than those who perform in local clubs. Soloists or headliners usually receive higher earnings than band members or opening acts. The most successful musicians earn performance or recording fees that far exceed the median earnings.

According to the American Federation of Musicians, weekly minimum salaries in major orchestras ranged from about $700 to $2,080 during the 2004–2005 performing season. Each orchestra works out a separate contract with its local union, but individual musicians may negotiate higher salaries. Top orchestras usually have a season ranging from twenty-four to fifty-two weeks, with eighteen orchestras reporting fifty-two-week contracts. Minimum salaries are often lower in regional orchestras, because fewer performances are scheduled. Regional orchestra musicians often are paid for their services without any guarantee of future employment. Community orchestras often have even more limited levels of funding and offer salaries that are much lower for seasons of shorter duration.

Although musicians employed by some symphony orchestras work under master wage agreements, which guarantee a season's work up to fifty-two weeks, many other musicians face relatively long periods of unemployment between jobs. Even when employed, many musicians and singers work part-time in unrelated occupations. Thus, their earnings usually are lower than earnings in many other occupations. Moreover, because they may not work steadily for one employer, some performers cannot qualify for unemployment compensation, and few have typical benefits such as sick leave or paid vacations. For these reasons, many musicians give private lessons or take jobs unrelated to music to supplement their earnings as performers.

Many musicians belong to a local of the American Federation of Musicians. Professional singers who perform live often belong to a branch of the American Guild of Musical Artists; those who record for the broadcast industries may belong to the American Federation of Television and Radio Artists.

Meet Some Music Professionals

Several music professionals have shared their experiences in personal accounts. Read on to find out what the life of a musician is really like.

Mark Marek, Singer and Dance Band Leader

Mark Marek is a singer and the leader of Private Stock Variety Dance Band of Lenexa, Kansas. His background includes two years of college with course work focusing on music theory, audio engineering, and the fundamentals of music and business.

Mark started playing drums in junior high school and later learned to play the six-string guitar. By age sixteen, he joined his brother's band, and nearly twenty years ago he started a band of his own. Mark describes Private Stock as "a country club, high dollar–type band." The band plays mostly at weddings, country clubs, and other formal occasions.

The band's working hours are usually 6:30 P.M. until 1:00 A.M., mostly on Fridays and Saturdays. Most jobs last three to four hours, but the band members must arrive at least an hour and a half before the start time to set up their instruments. They generally perform one-hour sets, with a twenty-minute break every hour or so. After the job, they have to stay to break down the equipment. Since the members have performed together for so many years, they don't need to rehearse more frequently than once every three or four months.

"I love seeing the reaction of the audience," Mark says. "It's fun to know and see that they are having a good time. That's the thrill I get out of it. What I least like is the inconsistency in bookings. Each month the number of gigs changes, which affects the cash flow. The peak periods for the band are December, May, and June."

There is also a business side to managing a band, and Mark spends weekdays taking bookings, arranging schedules, and making telephone calls. He also handles the contracts for each performance. In addition to his work with Private Stock, Mark gives private guitar lessons and books jobs for other bands.

Mark Marek offers some advice to anyone interested in a career similar to his. "To approach success in the music industry, you need to have good people skills, a general sense of business, a real enjoyment for what you do, a recognition of what your niche is in the music world, patience, good customer relations skills, expert technical skills, and a knowledge of audio and video technology.

"Having a band is a business, not an ego trip. You really need to have a basic knowledge of business and marketing," he stresses. "You can be the best musician, but you have to know how to sell yourself in order to be successful. It's a tough way to make a living. That's why you have to really have a passion for the business."

Priscilla Gale, Singer and Voice Teacher

Soprano Priscilla Gale attended both the Juilliard School of Music and the Cleveland Institute of Music. She has also studied in Austria and with private teachers Luigi Ricci (in Rome) and Michael Trimble. When she's not performing with an opera company or symphony orchestra, Priscilla teaches voice at Wesleyan University in Middletown, Connecticut.

Priscilla comes from a family of musicians, including pianists, singers, and violinists. She began playing the piano at age five. Despite assumptions that she would pursue a career as a pianist, Priscilla discovered that her real enjoyment was singing. Once she discovered opera, she knew that she had found her calling. Her first professional singing contract was with the Fort Wayne Symphony Orchestra during her senior year at the Cleveland Institute of Music.

Priscilla tries to explain a somewhat ethereal quality of singing. She says, "Every engagement you experience as a singer or performer changes you in the most wonderful way. You, as an artist, grow on multiple levels, both personally and artistically. Each time, your artistic life is changed; you grow in some immeasurable, wonderful way, and the possibilities are limitless."

Working conditions differ at various engagements. Priscilla describes opera rehearsals as intense, usually including ten- to twelve-hour days for two or three weeks. Performances with orchestras generally last over a three- or four-day period. The singer usually has a piano rehearsal with the conductor, then one or two orchestra rehearsals, followed by the performances.

Professional singers must be able to adapt to different working conditions. As Priscilla says, "It is always busy and intense but exciting. It is fast paced, and you must know your craft. There is little room for poor preparation. And you must always have the ability to adjust to every circumstance and environment, for no two are ever the same. Every conductor is different, every director, and so forth. You must be very adaptable and professional."

Like many dedicated performers, Priscilla gains an intensely personal satisfaction from her work while remaining aware of the realities of the profession. She says, "What I love most about my work is the ability to touch an audience—people I never meet individually, but collectively. My heart and soul meet theirs. But there are just not enough performance opportunities for everyone, and it is no longer possible to make a full-time living at this career unless you are one of the lucky top 20 percent."

Priscilla's experience allows her to offer some sound advice to aspiring singers. "I always tell people who want to do this kind of work to look inward and ask if there is anything else in life that will bring them happiness and fulfillment," she explains. "If so, then I suggest that they do that instead. If not, then they should by all means pursue this career. But know that it is—especially in the beginning—a very complicated business that represents a difficult life.

"Talent is but a small piece of it. Most people cannot comprehend the level of sacrifice that this career requires. There is that wonderful, romantic notion of being the 'starving artist,' but there's nothing romantic about it when you're living it.

"However, with hard work, determination, perseverance, and an unwavering faith in yourself, anything can happen. The journey is an incredible ride, and one I would not have missed. And as I look back at my past, at my present, and toward my future, I can honestly say that I am one of the lucky ones."

Karen Tyler, Singer, Songwriter, and Guitarist

Karen Tyler of Austin, Texas, earned an associate of arts degree from Pepperdine University in Malibu, California. She has been working as a blues singer, songwriter, and guitarist since 1979.

Karen has released three CDs, *Lovin' the Blues Too Long* (1997), *Alone & Blue* (2000), and *All Shades of Blue* (2003). The Karen Tyler Band won first-place honors in the 2003 Monterey Bay Blues Festival's Battle of the Bands after competing with 150 other bands.

"I had a natural talent for singing and found songwriting to be an incredible emotional outlet," says Karen. "And I have developed some pretty good business skills in order to stay in the music business. From the beginning, being front and center stage and being appreciated for my feelings was important to me."

Karen explains that while many artists have to work at other jobs to support their music, she was fortunate not to have to pursue other jobs. Early in her career she and her husband moved to Texas so that they could afford to live on one salary while Karen worked on her music. In 1998 they returned to California, where Karen formed her band. She writes the songs for the band and plays both lead and rhythm guitar; she also provides vocals.

Between performing and managing the band, Karen maintains a very full schedule. She keeps a mailing list, creates her own promotional materials, and writes a quarterly newsletter. She handles bookkeeping and accounting of band income and CD and tape sales. Karen also makes demo tapes and mails out promotional packages. To do the best job possible, she does a great deal of research on radio stations, booking agents, clubs, festivals, record companies, and any other aspects of the industry that will promote her music.

"I spend anywhere from one to four hours a day doing just the business of music," Karen says. "In addition, I play several nights a week from two to four hours, sometimes traveling three and four hours to play. Nothing at all may happen for a period of time, and just when I get into a routine I really like, someone will call or an opportunity will arise that will take all of my attention."

Karen acknowledges that the business side of her career often takes precedence over performing. "There is never a time when something like songwriting or practicing guitar doesn't take a back seat to some kind of business duty," she says. "I have tried to get a manager but have had some really bad experiences, and at this point in my career I feel that it is better if I retain the control, even if the responsibilities are a bit overwhelming. Everyone always has a suggestion about what you should be doing to help your career. And you can't possibly do everything people suggest, so making an action plan and sticking to it is the best thing. Trying to be organized is my biggest challenge, and getting things down on paper helps.

"I spend anywhere from twenty-five to thirty hours a week doing music business and play anywhere from four to twelve hours a week. I work from a home office, and so it gets a little lonely. My husband is moving his office into the home, which I assume will make it a bit better for me. At least I will have someone to bounce some ideas off. Sometimes I really feel like I'm out there all alone."

Karen talks about the ups and downs of her career. "I enjoy a good crowd response to my music," she says. "It makes it all worthwhile when someone comes up and tells me I have an amazing voice or that I play the guitar well or that a certain song really touched them.

"The worst part is probably that people don't go out as much as they used to. They are programmed by television, radio, and print media as to what to buy and what to listen to or go to see. They get comfortable going to hear certain acts and until they have heard rave reviews about someone forty or fifty times, they don't make the effort to go and see them. Even when they do, they are liable to slip back into the habit of going where they always go. A side effect is that talent doesn't count as much as who you know and how much fun you are to hang out with.

"On top of that, bands who want to 'make it' are expected to finance their own recordings, put out expensive CDs, and sell literally thousands of them before a record company will consider signing them. This is kind of hard when you are playing for fewer and fewer people every day."

Karen's advice for aspiring singer/songwriters addresses the practical side of the business. "I would advise those interested in this career to go to college and develop a talent (preferably nonmusical) whereby you can create your own business—computers, catering, consulting," she says. "You have to have some way of supporting yourself and coming up with $5,000 to $10,000 every year or two for a CD, and you have to have a flexible schedule so that you can tour and support the CD and work whenever you can."

Kathryn Maffei, Pianist and Music Director

Kathryn Maffei has been playing the piano for more than forty years. She has ten years of classical training through a concert pianist. Kathryn is currently music director at Our Lady of Miracles Church and School in Gustine, California.

"When I started taking piano lessons at eight years old," says Kathryn, "I began to entertain my family. Then I performed for family and friends' parties as well as local club and organization events. Quickly it spread to playing the piano for chorus classes in grammar school and high school bands and entertaining for many different kinds of local events, such as proms, fashion or variety shows, plays, and other social functions."

After her marriage, Kathryn took a few years off to raise her family. When her children began to attend school, she went with them to teach music classes, since none of the teachers at their school had musical abilities. Kathryn became the church organist and played at weddings, funerals, and masses.

As her music became known throughout the community, Kathryn began performing at parties at hotels and country clubs, as well as at parties celebrating holidays, birthdays, anniversaries, and class reunions, among other events. She became music director for a local performing arts company and has been piano conductor for over a dozen musical plays, including *Oliver*; *Annie*; *Big River*; *Hello Dolly*; *Bye Bye Birdie*; *Peter Pan*; *You're a Good Man, Charlie Brown*; and *Beauty and the Beast*.

Kathryn has also performed for a large number of fund-raising benefits, and she has served as a judge for local music talent showcases. In addition to her work as music director, Kathryn teaches private piano students and serves as the church's pianist and organist.

Kathryn began working at Our Lady of Miracles thirteen years ago, when the assistant superintendent of schools saw her perform and hired her immediately to teach music at her school. She currently teaches on Mondays and Wednesdays, working from 7:30 A.M. to 3:00 P.M. and has also served on a visual and performing arts committee to integrate performing arts into the diocesan schools.

"When designing music programs for children, my main concern is to teach a love for the art of music," Kathryn says. "I believe this is best accomplished at the earliest age possible. Hopefully, this is a feeling that will stay with the children all their lives, as it did in mine. It is well known that bringing music and liberal arts to students is important on so many levels and ensures a broad and rich education. The arts reinforce social skills, instill positive attitudes and values, and support growth and intellectual enrichment. The arts serve not only to develop personal intellectual growth, but also to sharpen judgment and interpersonal decision making. The key is to start with young children, and I know almost no other way to get and keep a small child's attention than with music.

"I truly love children and music and have never regretted my profession because I get so much enjoyment out of it. It is my life's work as much it would be for an accountant who works with numbers and a lawyer who deals with laws. To others I say, 'Go for it if you feel it is in your heart!'"

Mike Watson, Recording Artist

Mike Watson, head of Watson Entertainment, is a Georgia-based recording artist. He majored in music at West Georgia College. Mike performs regularly with his group, the Mike Watson Band, which has released the CD *Biscuit on My Mind*. He is also a successful producer and will soon open a music production facility for songwriters and artists in Nashville, Tennessee.

"I started playing professionally in 1980 as lead guitarist and harmony singer for a band on the circuit," says Mike. "I have been fascinated with music as long as I can remember, and I turned that dream into reality with a lot of hard work and perseverance and never settling for second best or taking no for an answer."

A typical day for Mike usually means rising at noon and spending time doing chores and running errands. He performs from 9 P.M. until 1 or 2 A.M. "Entertaining is what I do," he says. "Naturally, it is always a party atmosphere. When I go to different states doing shows, it's similar except I get to see places and people in one day I probably would never meet and maybe never see again.

"I love almost every part of my job and consider myself to be so very fortunate because I am able to do the one thing I love doing most—making a living at making music. My least favorite part is dealing with people who had too much to drink and every now and then having to deal with less than desirable booking agents who send you to a job that isn't quite what they paint it to be."

Like many artists, Mike believes success comes from following your dreams. "My advice to others is, if you have a genuine dream, never give up," Mike says. "If you know in your heart that you have what it takes to succeed in your chosen profession, go for it!"

Chris Murphy, Musician, Record Producer, and Disc Jockey

Chris Murphy is a professional musician, entertainer, record producer, and entertainment buyer, as well as a part-time disc jockey. He began music lessons as a teenager, and later he attended

Berkley College of Music in Boston. His father was also a musician, and Chris often played in bands with him before going on the road with his own band in 1978.

Chris has released two solo CDs, *I'm a Happy Guy* (2004) and *Blowin' the Horn* (1999), and has also performed on over a dozen CDs with other artists. He also manages Speakeasy CDs, an independent recording label for blues artists, and cohosts a radio show in Ontario called "Blues Never Die."

"I don't know how to do anything else," says Chris. "Music is one of the few things I was good at and could take pride in. As a teenager, I felt that music stood out as something that was fun and that I excelled at. I started playing the saxophone at age seventeen and started playing in bands about the same time. I was in love with the blues long before I became a blues musician."

Chris loves the atmosphere of performing in blues clubs four to six nights a week. He spends time daily on the phone, organizing shows and musicians' schedules. Overall, his feelings about his career are positive. As Chris says, "I meet a lot of interesting, talented, and funny people. I receive a lot of respect and love from the audiences I perform for. There is nothing that can replace the feeling of being onstage with a great band on a good night! I also have time to spend with my daughter in the daytime during the week, though occasionally I am away for the weekend.

"I enjoy the fact that when I go out to earn money, I am going out to play. How many people can say that?

"My advice to others is to never, ever quit. The people who hang in there are the ones who inherit the entertainment business."

Lionel Ward, Musician

Lionel Ward first became interested in being a musician when he was only nine years old and his mother bought him an Airline guitar for Christmas. Now he tours North America and Europe as the lead singer for the New World Band, an Elvis-tribute group. Lionel was discovered by the late Wolfman Jack, who noticed Lionel's resemblance to Elvis Presley and invited him to a meeting. Lionel's manager then sent a demo tape to Wolfman Jack's record label, Sonic Records, and the New World Band began recording under the Sonic label. Lionel and the band have released three CDs: *This One's for You, Rockabilly Rebel,* and *All the Girls.*

"I came from a musical family, so there was always music in the house," Lionel says. "Music is therapy for the soul. It is the greatest feeling in the world to be able to play in front of an audience and see the enjoyment you give people. If you can relieve them of the everyday burdens of life for just a few minutes, you've done something important. The natural high you get from doing a live show cannot be compared to anything else. The only way you can achieve this feeling is through the music. And the beautiful thing is that it is all natural. Being able to sing and play an instrument is a God-given talent; you cannot buy this anywhere. You have to be born with it. It is a blessing to be able to share it with your audience."

Lionel stresses how important it is for a performer to give his or her all to every audience. "One thing I learned very early in the entertainment business is that every performance has to be the best you can possibly do," he says. "The key is to be able to sing your songs as if they are being performed for the very first time. It may actually be the thousandth time you have sung that song, but in my opinion, it should be a thousand times better than the first. The people in the audience have chosen to take the time out of their evening to come and hear you play. You do not want to disappoint them, and I always make sure I do my very best, whether there are five people in the audience or five thousand."

In addition to performing, Lionel's role as lead singer means that he is responsible for seeing that all necessary arrangements are made for the band. He determines which lighting and pubic address systems will be used and how large a road crew will be needed. Such details are important for a successful performance.

"I must ensure that all of this is taken care of," Lionel says, "because it affects my show tremendously if I cannot hear the band or we can't see the audience because someone forgot to put up a spotlight."

Lionel acknowledges that it is difficult to describe a typical workday in his career. "As far as what work I actually do," he says, "I am involved with every aspect, right down to the last microphone sound check. You cannot measure how many hours are involved because some shows take days. If you count the actual rehearsal time, driving to the gigs, set up and tear down times, and sound checks, you would think we were insane. Our lives are devoted to music, but it is a labor of love. Sometimes we are gone from our homes for weeks. Living in hotels, doing radio and television interviews, is not one big party. I am very fortunate because for as long as I have been doing this, I have never considered it work. I truly love what I am doing.

"I particularly enjoy recording in the studio because it's like taking a piece of your life and freezing it in time. But I also love performing live. Again, there is no better feeling in the world than when the audience is wrapped up in your song and you are taking them on a journey.

"As far as I can see, there is no downside in this business. I am very fortunate that my wife travels with me and shares my dreams. For some people, I think a downside would be having to leave their family."

Lionel offers encouraging advice to aspiring performers. "My advice to others is to follow your dreams and what you feel in your heart. This business is very rough and unforgiving at times. But if you believe in yourself and you have the burning desire to make it, then you will. This business cannot be measured by hours or even days. It cannot be measured by money, either, though we need money to survive. If you truly believe in yourself and your music, everything else will fall into place.

"Many times you will hear me thank the audience for their support through the years. I was born a poor boy—rich with love and dreams, though—and I am definitely living my dreams!"

Dancers

The dance is a poem of which each movement is a word.

—Mata Hari

Ever since ancient times, dancers have used their bodies to express ideas, stories, rhythm, and sound. In addition to being an art form for its own sake, dance also complements opera, musical comedy, television, movies, music videos, and commercials. Therefore, many dancers sing and act as well as dance.

Career Opportunities

Dancers most often perform as a group, although a few top artists dance solo. Many dancers combine stage work with teaching or choreographing.

- **Choreographer.** Choreographers create original dances. They may also create new interpretations of traditional dances, such as the *Nutcracker* ballet. Choreographers instruct performers at rehearsals to achieve the desired effect. They also audition all of the performers.
- **Ballet Dancer.** Ballet dancing requires a lot of training—in fact, more than any other kind of dancing. Ballet dancers are performers who express a theme or story.
- **Modern Dancer.** Modern dancers use bodily movements and facial expressions to express ideas and moods. Jazz is one area of modern dance.
- **Tap Dancer.** Tap dancers use tap shoes to keep time with all kinds of music by tapping out various dance rhythms.

The Life of a Dancer

Dancing is strenuous. Rehearsals require very long hours and usually take place daily, including weekends and holidays. For shows on the road, weekend travel is often necessary. Rehearsals and practice are generally scheduled during the day. Since most performances take place in the evening, dancers must usually work late hours.

Due to the physical demands, most dancers stop performing by their late thirties, but they sometimes continue to work in the dance field as choreographers, dance teachers and coaches, or artistic directors. Some celebrated dancers, however, continue performing beyond the age of fifty.

Dancers work in a variety of settings, including eating and drinking establishments, theatrical and television productions, dance studios and schools, dance companies and bands, and amusement parks. In addition, there are many dance instructors in secondary schools, colleges and universities, and private studios. Many teachers also perform from time to time.

New York City is the home of many of the major dance companies. Other cities with full-time professional dance companies include Atlanta, Boston, Chicago, Cincinnati, Cleveland, Columbus, Dallas, Houston, Miami, Milwaukee, Philadelphia, Pittsburgh, Salt Lake City, San Francisco, Seattle, and Washington, D.C.

Training and Qualifications

Training for dancers varies according to the type of dance. Early ballet training for women usually begins at five to eight years of age and is often given by private teachers and independent ballet schools. Serious training traditionally begins between the ages of ten and twelve. Men usually begin their training between the ages of ten and fifteen.

Students who demonstrate potential in the early teens receive more intensive and advanced professional training at regional ballet schools or schools conducted under the auspices of the major ballet companies.

Leading dance school companies often have summer training programs from which they select candidates for admission to their regular, full-time training programs. Most dancers have their professional auditions by age seventeen or eighteen; however, training and practice never end. Professional ballet dancers have lessons that last one to one and one-half hours every day and spend many additional hours practicing and rehearsing.

Early and intensive training also is important for the modern dancer, but modern dance generally does not require as many years of training as ballet. Because of the strenuous and time-consuming training required, a dancer's formal academic instruction may be minimal. However, a broad, general education including music, literature, history, and the visual arts is helpful in the interpretation of dramatic episodes, ideas, and feelings.

Many colleges and universities offer bachelor's or higher degrees in dance. This might be through the departments of music, physical education, fine arts, or theater. Most programs concentrate on modern dance but also offer courses in ballet and classical techniques, dance composition, dance history, dance criticism, and movement analysis.

A college education is not essential to obtaining employment as a professional dancer. In fact, ballet dancers who postpone their first audition until graduation may compete at a disadvantage with younger dancers. On the other hand, a college degree can help the dancer who retires at an early age, as often happens, and wishes to enter another field of work.

Completion of a college program in dance and education is essential to qualify for employment as a college, elementary, or high school dance teacher. Colleges, as well as conservatories, generally require graduate degrees, but performance experience often may be substituted. A college background is not necessary for teaching dance privately or choreographing professionally. Studio schools usually require teachers to have experience as performers.

Earnings for Dancers

Earnings of dancers at many of the largest companies and in commercial settings are governed by union contracts. Dancers in the major opera ballet, classical ballet, and modern dance corps belong to the American Guild of Musical Artists of the AFL-CIO; those who appear on live or videotaped television programs belong to the American Federation of Television and Radio Artists; those who perform in films and on television belong to the Screen Actors Guild; and those in musical theater are members of the Actors' Equity Association. The unions and producers sign basic agreements specifying minimum salary rates, hours of work, benefits, and other conditions of employment. However, the contract each dancer signs with the producer of the show may be more favorable than the basic agreement.

Median hourly earnings of dancers were $8.54 in May 2004. The middle 50 percent earned between $6.71 and $15.62. The lowest 10 percent earned less than $5.87, and the highest 10 percent earned more than $21.59.

Annual earnings data for dancers are not available because the wide variation in the number of hours worked by dancers and the short-term nature of many jobs (which may last for one day or one week) make it extremely rare for dancers to have guaranteed employment that exceeds three to six months. Median hourly earnings in the industries employing the largest number of dancers were as follows: performing arts companies, $14.82; schools, $14.94; amusement and recreation industries, $7.68; and establishments serving alcohol, $6.78.

Dancers who were on tour usually received an additional allowance for room and board, as well as extra compensation for overtime. Earnings from dancing are usually low because employment is part year and irregular. Dancers often supplement their income by working as guest artists with other dance companies, teaching dance, or taking jobs unrelated to the field.

Median annual earnings of salaried choreographers were $33,670 in May 2004. The middle 50 percent earned between $21,530 and $48,940. The lowest 10 percent earned less than $14,980, and the highest 10 percent earned more than $68,190.

Median annual earnings were $34,090 in "other schools and instruction," a North American Industry Classification System category that includes dance studios and schools.

Most salaried dancers and choreographers covered by union contracts receive some paid sick leave and various health and pension benefits, including extended sick pay and family-leave benefits provided by their unions. Employers contribute toward these benefits. Dancers and choreographers not covered by union contracts usually do not enjoy such benefits.

For More Information

There are many sources of additional information about careers in the performing arts.

Acting

Information about opportunities in regional theaters may be obtained from:

Theatre Communications Group (TCG)
520 Eighth Avenue, Twenty-Fourth Floor
New York, NY 10018
www.tcg.org

A directory of theatrical programs may be purchased from:

National Association of Schools of Theatre (NAST)
11250 Roger Bacon Drive, Suite 21
Reston, VA 20190
http://nast.arts-accredit.org

For additional information, contact the following associations:

Actors' Equity Association
165 West Forty-Sixth Street
New York, NY 10036
www.actorsequity.org

Alliance of Canadian Cinema, Television, and Radio Artists
  (ACTRA)
625 Church Street, Third Floor
Toronto, ON M4Y 2G1
Canada
www.actra.ca

Alliance of Resident Theaters
575 Eighth Avenue, Suite 17 South
New York, NY 10018
www.offbroadwayonline.com

American Federation of Television and Radio Artists (AFTRA)
260 Madison Avenue
New York, NY 10016
www.aftra.org

American Film Institute
2021 North Western Avenue
Los Angeles, CA 90027
www.afi.com

American Theatre Works, Inc.
PO Box 510
Dorset, VT 05251
www.dorsettheatrefestival.com

Americans for the Arts
1000 Vermont Avenue NW, Sixth Floor
Washington, DC 20005
www.artsusa.org

Canadian Actors' Equity Association
44 Victoria Street, Twelfth Floor
Toronto, ON M5C 3C4
Canada
www.caea.com

Screen Actors Guild (SAG)
5757 Wilshire Boulevard
Los Angeles, CA 90036
www.sag.org

Music

There are literally hundreds of professional associations for musicians. Contact any of the following organizations for more information about employment in this field.

Academy of Country Music (ACM)
4100 West Alameda Avenue, Suite 208
Burbank, CA 91505
www.acmcountry.com

American Choral Directors Association (ACDA)
545 Couch Drive
Oklahoma City, OK 73102
www.acdaonline.org

American Federation of Musicians (AFM)
1501 Broadway, Suite 600
New York, NY 10036
www.afm.org

American Federation of Television and Radio Artists (AFTRA)
260 Madison Avenue
New York, NY 10016
www.aftra.org

American Guild of Music (AGM)
PO Box 599
Warren, MI 48090
www.americanguild.org

American Guild of Musical Artists (AGMA)
1430 Broadway, Fourteenth Floor
New York, NY 10018
www.musicalartists.org

American Guild of Organists (AGO)
475 Riverside Drive, Suite 1260
New York, NY 10115
www.agohq.org

American Music Conference (AMC)
5790 Armada Drive
Carlsbad, CA 92008
www.amc-music.org

American Musicological Society
201 South Thirty-Fourth Street
University of Pennsylvania
Philadelphia, PA 19104
www.ams-net.org

American Symphony Orchestra League (ASOL)
33 West Sixtieth Street, Fifth Floor
New York, NY 10023
www.symphony.org

Broadcast Education Association (BEA)
1771 N Street NW
Washington, DC 20036
www.beaweb.org

Broadcast Music, Inc. (BMI)
320 West Fifty-Seventh Street
New York, NY 10019
www.bmi.com

Chamber Music America
305 Seventh Avenue
New York, NY 10001
www.chamber-music.org

Chorus America
1156 Fifteenth Street, Suite 310
Washington, DC 20005
www.chorusamerica.org

College Music Society
312 East Pine Street
Missoula, MT 59802
www.music.org

Concert Artists Guild (CAG)
850 Seventh Avenue, Suite 1205
New York, NY 10019
www.concertartists.org

Country Music Association (CMA)
One Music Circle South
Nashville, TN 37203
www.cmaworld.com

Gospel Music Association (GMA)
1205 Division Street
Nashville, TN 37203
www.gospelmusic.org

Metropolitan Opera Association (MOA)
Lincoln Center
New York, NY 10023
www.metoperafamily.org

National Academy of Popular Music (NAPM)
www.songwritershalloffame.org

National Academy of Recording Arts and Sciences (NARAS)
3401 Pico Boulevard
Santa Monica, CA 90405
www.grammy.com

National Association of Schools of Music (NASM)
11250 Roger Bacon Drive, Suite 21
Reston, VA 20190
http://nasm.arts-accredit.org

National Symphony Orchestra Association (NSOA)
JFK Center for the Performing Arts
2700 F Street NW
Washington, DC 20566
www.kennedy-center.org/nso/nsoed/misc.html

Opera America
330 Seventh Avenue, Sixteenth Floor
New York, NY 10001
www.operaamerica.org

Radio-Television News Directors Association Canada
2175 Sheppard Avenue East, Suite 310
Toronto, ON M2J 1W8
Canada
www.rtndacanada.com

Society of Professional Audio Recording Services
9 Music Square South, Suite 222
Nashville, TN 37203
www.spars.com

Women in Music
PO Box 1215
Old Chelsea Station
New York, NY 10113
www.womeninmusic.org

Dance

For information about colleges and universities that teach dance,
including details on the types of courses offered and scholarships,
contact:

National Dance Association (NDA)
American Alliance for Health, Physical Education, Recreation,
    & Dance
1900 Association Drive
Reston, VA 20191
www.aahperd.org/nda

A directory of dance, art and design, music, and theater programs may be obtained from:

National Association of Schools of Dance (NASD)
11250 Roger Bacon Drive, Suite 21
Reston, VA 20190
http://nasd.arts-accredit.org

For information on all aspects of dance, including job listings, contact:

American Dance Guild
PO Box 2006
Lenox Hill Station
New York, NY 10021
www.americandanceguild.org

A directory of dance companies and related organizations, plus other information on professional dance, is available from:

Dance/USA
1111 Sixteenth Street NW, Suite 300
Washington, DC 20036
www.danceusa.org

About the Author

Jan Goldberg's love for the printed page began well before her second birthday. Regular visits to the book bindery where her grandfather worked produced a magic combination of sights and smells that she carries with her to this day.

Childhood was filled with composing poems and stories, reading books, and playing library. Elementary and high school included an assortment of contributions to school newspapers. While a full-time college student, Goldberg wrote extensively as part of her job responsibilities in the College of Business Administration at Roosevelt University in Chicago. After receiving a degree in elementary education, she was able to extend her love of reading and writing to her students.

Goldberg has written extensively in the occupations area for General Learning Corporation's *Career World Magazine*, as well as for the many career publications produced by CASS Communications. She has also contributed to a number of projects for educational publishers, including Scott Foresman, Addison-Wesley, and Camp Fire Boys and Girls.

As a feature writer, Goldberg's work has appeared in *Parenting*, *Today's Chicago Woman*, *Opportunity Magazine*, *North Shore Magazine*, *Correspondent*, *Chicago Parent*, *Successful Student*, *Complete Woman*, and the Pioneer Press newspapers. In all, she has published more than 250 pieces as a freelance writer.

In addition to *Careers for Competitive Spirits*, she is the author of more than a dozen career books published by McGraw-Hill. She also recently completed four Capstone High/Low Books for elementary school students: *Private Investigator*, *Fire Fighter*, *Medical Record Technician*, and *Security Guard*.